You Are Here

You Are Here

Keywords for Life Explorers

David Steindl-Rast

Founder, A Network for Grateful Living

with Mario Quintana

ORBIS BOOKS
www.orbisbooks.com

ORBIS BOOKS
www.orbisbooks.com

Fathers and Brothers
MARYKNOLL

Founded in 1970, Orbis Books endeavors to publish works that enlighten the mind, nourish the spirit, and challenge the conscience. The publishing arm of the Maryknoll Fathers and Brothers, Orbis seeks to explore the global dimensions of the Christian faith and mission, to invite dialogue with diverse cultures and religious traditions, and to serve the cause of reconciliation and peace. The books published reflect the views of their authors and do not represent the official position of the Maryknoll Society. To learn more about Maryknoll and Orbis Books, please visit our website at www.orbisbooks.com.

Library of Congress Cataloging-in-Publication Data

Names: Steindl-Rast, David, author.
Title: You are here : keywords for life explorers / David Steindl-Rast, founder, a network for Grateful Living.
Description: Maryknoll, New York : Orbis Books, [2023] | Includes bibliographical references and index. | Summary: "David Steindl-Rast advises those looking for a way to God to start by examining their own experience"— Provided by publisher.
Identifiers: LCCN 2022044937 (print) | LCCN 2022044938 (ebook) | ISBN 9781626985155 (print) | ISBN 9781608339778 (ebook)
Subjects: LCSH: Spirituality—Catholic Church. | Mindfulness (Psychology) —Religious aspects. | Gratitude--Religious aspects—Catholic Church.
Classification: LCC BX2350.65 .S753 2023 (print) | LCC BX2350.65 (ebook) | DDC 248.4/82—dc23/eng20230106
LC record available at https://lccn.loc.gov/2022044937
LC ebook record available at https://lccn.loc.gov/2022044938

To the young and to all those whose heart is young enough

to be passionately alive to the widest horizons.

Contents

Annotations to Some of Our Keywords

Note to the Reader

This is a book of keywords for the spiritual life. When you encounter a keyword in the text, it is marked with an asterisk to catch your attention. Some of these keywords are discussed in detail. The second part of this book offers summaries of all the other keywords, and when these appear in the alphabetical listing with an asterisk, it is to indicate that it's been introduced earlier in the book.

Introduction: The Big Picture

An Attempt at Getting the Whole into View

> *I want to know what this whole show is all about,*
> *before it's out.*
>
> *Piet Hein*

It is the big picture that interests me. Seeing the whole within its widest horizon. Understanding how everything is connected with everything—that has been the passion of my life. Being ninety-six years old now, I asked my young friend Thomas, who is in his twenties, "How about young people today? Do they—like myself and Danish poet Piet Hein—urgently 'want to know what this whole show is all about'?" "We wonder about it, *all the time*," he answered, without a moment's hesitation.

It was Tommy's answer that encouraged me to write this book. I want to offer to others signposts for orientation by sharing with them the most important insights I have gained in a lifetime. Only by looking at the dynamic interconnection of everything with everything can we hope to find our own place as human beings within the widest network of networks and understand our function within totality. That means no less than the attempt to sketch a stamp-size map of everything the mind can conceive. I can't blame anyone for calling this a foolhardy venture. But why not be venturesome?

The first objection to our plan will probably be, *How can you draw a map of something that's constantly changing?* What we are looking for cannot be seen on a static map. Our vision will have to include movement and change as the most obvious features of the big picture. But we can also become aware of a less obvious, though equally important feature of the whole: stillness.* Although everything is moving, and we are moving along with it, all is—at the same time at rest in itself, in its own inner stillness—"still and still moving" (T. S. Eliot). Stillness, therefore, as well as movement, belongs to the whole, and we will have to acknowledge both in the big picture we draw. But can we find an image for the whole of all there is—for "the whole show"—that expresses both movement and stillness in one? What comes to my mind is a circle dance. Everywhere in the world, young children enjoy holding hands in a circle, singing and moving to the rhythm* of their song. And not only children: sacred dancers of many ancient traditions also follow this pattern of a movement that rests in itself. As the big picture we might even imagine a circle dance without beginning or end.

No matter how dizzying the movement may sometimes become—think, for instance, of whirling dervishes—any dance remains still at rest in itself. And no matter how long the strides or leaps of the dancers, they do not move toward any destination. We do not dance in order to get somewhere. The dance isn't moving toward a goal, yet it does have a goal: perfect dancing. Thus, the dance metaphor shows us that the whole can, paradoxically, at the same time have and not have a goal. Its direction has no goal, but its performance does. Each movement is an end in itself; each reaches perfection* by being fully itself. As we share in life's dance, our goal is the perfection of being in step—now and now and now. What it "is all about" is one opportunity* after another to interact with all other dancers through the one partner next to you—to be in step, to be in tune with the universe.

In some great achievements of humanity—think of Handel's *Messiah*, the Taj Mahal, or any hidden act of human heroism— our way of dancing can even reach a perfection that expresses something as primordial and universal as an archetype. Rainer Maria Rilke sees this as a sort of homecoming of all that is fully matured into a kind of primeval and lasting relevance and contrasts it with the irrelevant drifting of wandering clouds.*

> *Swift though the world may shift shape*
> *as clouds change appearance,*
> *all that has fully matured*
> *joins the primeval.*

This homecoming to deep relevance can take place in the humblest actions of human love and caring. Every time a mother takes her baby to her heart, she reenacts the Great Mother, and every time a young man conquers his willfulness, the archetype of the sage lights up behind him.

Using a different image, the poet speaks of us humans as bees who harvest the nectar of the visible into the great golden honeycomb of the invisible. Whatever the concept—honeycomb or archetype—it is beautiful to think of a plane of existence on which every brave, compassionate, creative response to life—all that reaches fulfillment on the level of constant change—finds its way home to a deeper level on which it is preserved from getting lost forever.

Improvement of one's dancing is a personal task, but it is not a private matter; since everything hangs together with everything, the whole dance is affected by the way each dancer dances. The

---

* All quotations from Rilke are the author's own translations.

quality of the sacred circle dance depends on the attention each dancer pays to all others. Every attuned dance step improves the whole dance. William Butler Yeats knew this:

> *O body swayed to music, O brightening glance,*
> *How can we know the dancer from the dance?*
>
> *(from "Among School Children")*

C. S. Lewis, in whose space novel *Perelandra* I first encountered the image of the Great Dance—the Great Game, he also calls it—writes,

> It has begun from before always.... The dance which we dance is at the centre and for the dance all things were made.... In the plan of the Great Dance plans without number interlock, and each movement becomes in its season the breaking into flower of the whole design to which all else had been directed.... All that is made seems planless to the darkened mind, because there are more plans than it looked for.... Set your eyes on one movement and it will lead you through all patterns and it will seem to you the master movement. But the seeming will be true. Let no mouth open to gainsay it. There seems no plan because it is all plan: there seems no centre because it is all centre.[1]

T. S. Eliot speaks of the Now as "the still point of the turning world." That Now is the moment when the dancer is "still and still moving," perfectly in step with the cosmic rhythm.

Keep that dance metaphor for the big picture in mind. It will stand as background behind all the explorations in this book. In

---

[1] C. S. Lewis, *The Essential C. S. Lewis*, ed. Lyle W. Dorsett (New York: Scribner, 2017), 290–91.

a sense, the entire book is an exploration of the rich implications of this image. A more poetic title for the book might have been "How to Join the Great Dance." We quote poets often, because they can unlock unexpected treasures hidden in a word, phrase, or image. This is true also of the Great Dance as image for "this whole show."

A well-known Russian proverb says, "Love is like a ring; a ring has no ending." And Robert Frost adds,

> *We dance round in a ring and suppose,*
> *But the Secret sits in the middle and knows.*
>
> *("The Secret Sits")*

These two short texts taken together point in the same direction as Dante's celebrated verse: "Love that moves the sun and other stars." What "this whole show is all about"—the central Mystery of the Great Dance—is Love.*

Steps toward Orientation

1

Orientation

Our First Step

Friends told me about their two-year-old toddler: "When he wakes up in the morning, he first has to find his bearings, his orientation. We hear him talking to himself in his crib in the next room. He orientates himself by naming one object in his room after the other, repeating aloud a whole litany of newly learned words: 'blanket, lamp, teddy bear....'" Not only as children but throughout our lives, we use words to find our way through the maze of this bewildering world, and we need clearly defined words to get properly oriented.

The word "orientation," like "Orient," comes from the Latin *oriens,* which refers to the "sunrise," the "east." If we know the point where the sun rises, we can determine all other points of the compass and find the direction we want to take. Some words can help us in a similar way. Words full of light, they beam, as it were, like the floodlights of a lighthouse and build a bridge over troubled water. Such luminous words can also become keywords that unlock new insights* for us. We can learn "to think along language," the way we walk along a path through meadows, enjoying, flower by flower, ever-new discoveries as we go.

"Thinking along language" is a phrase that Martin Heidegger has coined. I have discovered the joy that springs from thinking along language and am learning to pay close attention to the insights of our ancestors who have left tracks in the language we inherited from them. Like us, they were trying to find their way in the world and in life; they too were looking for reliable coordinates for inner alignment and spiritual orientation. That is why there is a treasure of wisdom* and guidance hidden in the language they left us. And because poetry* condenses language many times over, poems reveal this treasure in its most pure and radiant manifestation.

We need all the help we can get to find orientation, but above all, we need to pay close attention to our own experience. Every journey starts with a first step, and our first step in orientating ourselves needs to be finding out who we are.

2

The I

My Existence as a Gift

My orientation in the world necessarily starts with where I am. "You are here," it says on the map at the entrance to a state park. That I am here, in this world, is the undeniable fact with which my orientation must begin. I can find no other starting point than this very personal one, because there is no other. But I can express this fundamental insight in two significantly different ways: "I exist," or "My existence is a given fact." The distinction between these two expressions can help us greatly to find our place in the Big Picture.

With the phrase "I exist," I affirm that my existence is a given fact. But I express this in the first-person singular as my one undeniable experience. To deny it would be self-contradictory, for unless I existed, I could not deny it. Thus my existence necessarily becomes the starting point for orienting myself in the world. But I can easily slip into mistaking this center of *my* world for the absolute center of the world altogether. When that happens, I begin to conceive of everything else as revolving around little me. The whole environment* of which I am part becomes merely *my* surroundings. An I that cannot go beyond seeing itself as the center of everything remains stuck in itself.

The second way to express the basic insight that I exist—"My existence is a given fact"—is formulated in the third-person singular. This point of grammar makes a significant difference. The subject of this new formulation is not my I, but my existence, and I am making a statement about it, as if I were an onlooker. By adopting this outsider's view, I avoid the risk of focusing only on myself. Rather, I see my existence as one fact among many, and as a *given* fact, at that. Thus I acknowledge my existence as a gift, a gift of the universe. This implies a give-and-take, and I begin to see my environment no longer merely as my surroundings. Instead, I find myself related to everything around me by a network* of relationships. This kind of self-understanding allows the healthy development of the "I myself*" through a multitude of relationships.

3

The Self

Our Shared Innermost Being

When I speak of my Self, I mean my innermost being. I am aware that I can "go into myself," into an inner realm that is accessible only to myself. Others can experience my body "from the outside," but only I can experience my "inside." I am some-body—some body—one body among other bodies. But usually we don't say, "I *am* a body," but rather, "I *have* a body." Isn't that strange, though, when you think about it? There is somebody—some body—saying, "I have a body." Who is speaking here? It is my embodied Self speaking—*as one* with my body—*about* my body as its visible manifestation. Inner and outer* cannot be separated, only distinguished. I mean the *embodied* Self when I say, "I myself."

But how can I clearly distinguish the I from the Self? Can I actually become aware of my Self, as distinct from my I? You might want to try an experiment in order to experience that distinction. Your reflective consciousness allows you to observe yourself. So, turn your mind's attention on yourself, sitting there and reading these lines. You need to distance yourself interiorly from the object of your observation. Look again at yourself with your inner eye. Do you somehow still see two: yourself as observed and yourself as the observer? If so, you need to try again until you focus exclusively on what you see with your mind's eye: yourself sitting and reading. You are no longer observing the observer; you *are* the observer. At this point you are experiencing your Self. The observer whom no one can observe is your Self.

As we look more closely, we discover various aspects of the Self: it is not bound by space nor by time, limitless and one indivisible whole. Let's look at these aspects one by one. First, like your mind,* the Self is *not bound by space*. Yet the Self is not identical with the mind. We say not only, "I have a body," but also, "I have a mind." Since the Self can observe both body and mind, it transcends both. Second, the Self is not restricted by time. When I remember my childhood, I find a different I, a childish one, not my current I. And yet I find in my memory* the same Self then, as it is now and always. That is also why friends meeting again after thirty years will recognize one another, even though not one cell in their bodies is the same. Third, not being restrained by space and time, the Self is *limitless*, yet it manifests itself through my I that is indeed limited by time and space and in many other ways. And finally, the Self is indivisible. Only what is subject to time or space can be divided. Since the Self is limitless, as we have seen, and also beyond my individual mind, it must be one for all of us. There is only one Self.

This has surprising implications for my relationships with others. Every I is unique. Not even our fingerprints match those of anyone else among billions of others. Yet all of us call the one indivisible Self, "*my*self." In everyone I encounter, I meet the one Self that is common to all of us. In the amazing double-realm* of this world, the one inexhaustible Self expresses itself again and again in still another I, and communicates through that one with all others. I differs from I in its uniqueness, but our Self is one and makes us one.

Do you remember the beginning of your very first friendship—possibly in kindergarten? Wasn't that a moment of overwhelming surprise: how can someone else be *so completely different* and at the same time *so me*? Not *like* me—the big difference between us is what makes the whole experience so exciting—and yet in the truest sense of the word, *me*! No wonder that one of the most beloved children's classics is titled *I'll Be You and You Be Me*.[1] The Greek philosopher Aristotle referred to this when he understood friendship as "a single soul* that lives in two bodies." There is "one Self" in all bodies, but the eyes of friends are open to this crucial fact, and they are aware of its importance in relation to each other. If not only friends but all of us could, once in a while at least, become aware of the fact that one Self unites us all, our world would be a friendlier place.

I have been privileged to meet people whose I seemed completely translucent, letting the Self shine through. In their presence, it becomes easier for me to be myself. At such moments, I'm aware of being a unique expression in space and time of the one great Self. Different traditions call the Self under this aspect by different names. For the Native American Pima people it is *I'itoi*; for Hindus, *Atman*; for Buddhists, *Buddha Nature*. Christians call it the *Christ within us*. St. Paul points to this when he writes, "I live, yet not I, Christ lives in me" (Galatians 2:20). To become ever more transparent for the Self in this sense is the great task of "becoming who we truly are."

That task involves "playing my role in life well," as we say. But what does that mean? This role is not a fixed script, and playing it means improvising—as in improvisational acting, or, to use a different image, as in playing jazz. In jazz, the music is constantly unfolding and unpredictably changing, as each player listens and responds to all others. What each one can contribute

---

[1] Ruth Krauss, *I'll Be You and You Be Me*, pictures by Maurice Sendak (1954; New York: HarperCollins, 2001).

is determined by this player's instrument, with all its possibilities and limitations. The instrument you are given, by birth, determines your contribution far more than you might at first suspect. Determining factors, not under your control, are the time and place of your birth—of your entrance onto the big stage of the world, where the play has been going on for a long time, before you joined it. And think of the strengths and weaknesses of the body and mind with which you were born, of the talents and shortcomings you have inherited. Regardless of the way you deal with those givens, they will go a long way to determining the possibilities and limits of your improvisation. Your way of "playing well" cannot depend on *what* instrument you play; it must depend on *how* you play it.

"What are the standards, then," you will ask, "by which I shall measure how well I'm playing?" The answer that suggests itself from what we've seen about the Self is this: You must play as yourself—as your Self. How well you play your role in life does not depend on your talents or the lack of them, but on becoming more and more transparent for the Self, as in your best moments. That means remaining aware that we—the players—are all one Self, and acting in such a way that you affirm our mutual belonging. Your acting—all your actions—express a "lived Yes to belonging." This is our definition of love: a radically lived "Yes!" to mutual belonging. Thus, "playing your role well" means expressing, through everything you do in your life, love.

This means no less than fulfilling the great biblical commandment, "Love your neighbor as yourself" (Leviticus 19:18). Not "*like* yourself," but "*as* yourself"—since your Self is your neighbor's Self as well. In all the other players, you encounter our common Self—even in your enemies. Therefore, "Love your enemies" (Matthew 5:44) is not a self-contradictory command. For instance, all who destroy the rainforest remain my enemies, even though I strive to love them. If my love made them my friends, I could no longer love my enemies. I do everything I can to counteract their efforts and to take away their power to do harm, but love makes me show them the respect that every human being deserves and treat them the way I'd want them to treat me, if our roles were reversed. In my fiercely determined opposition, I must never forget that their Self is my Self.

There is only one Self. To forget this fact amounts to forgetting that it is ultimately the Self that—through its countless manifestations—plays *all* the roles on the world stage. When I forget that, I become like an actor so lost in my role that, in the end, I can no longer distinguish myself from my role. To the extent to which this happens, my I loses awareness of the Self and, by doing so, becomes an Ego.

4

The Ego

When the I Forgets the Self

Ego is simply the Latin word for "I," but we'll be using it with a negative connotation because we need a word for the I when it loses—partly or completely—awareness of the Self. The more the I forgets the Self that makes it one with all others, the more it feels isolated and becomes the Ego.

Using a somewhat whimsical metaphor, I spoke of the Self as playing *all* the roles in the great world theater. We might think of a puppeteer, who is behind every character on her little stage. If she performs with hand puppets, she may have one hand inside the princess, and the other hand inside the dragon threatening the princess. Knowing this will certainly make me less frightened, if I happen to be the princess. I will trust the puppeteer. But any puppet that forgets the puppeteer is bound to imagine that it is merely one empty skin among countless others, and some of them look anything but friendly. It will be scared. When we forget that one and the same Self is holding us together, we actors on the world stage will feel a frightening sense of isolation. Our trust is likely to flip over into fear. And fear is the cause for everything that goes wrong in the big show.

Fear makes the Ego aggressive. It seeks security through gaining power over others, through trying to work its way up over everyone else, through suppressing others and exploiting them. The Ego is afraid that there is not enough to go around for so many; that's why it becomes greedy, stingy, and jealous. It has lost its orientation and has become the center around which all its thinking and striving is revolving. It gets more and more entangled in a fear-ridden society in which Ego collides with Ego, a society—our own, unfortunately!—that is characterized by hunger for power, by violence, greed, and exploitation—and all of this out of fear.*

How can an Ego that is lost and entangled like that find its way out and recover the right relationship to the Self? The answer is this: since the Ego has become lost through forgetfulness and fear, it can find its way home through the opposite of these two: mindfulness* and trust.* In its innermost heart, the Ego never fully forgets the Self—the puppeteer—but its memory is dulled, as in sleep. The Ego can be aroused from that sleep and return home to the Self—becoming "I myself" again, like Ebenezer Scrooge in Charles Dickens's *A Christmas Carol.*

It is important to remember that the Ego is not a third entity in addition to the I and the Self. The Ego always remains the I, but it is an I all shriveled up, because it lacks the expansive awareness of the Self that unites it with every other I.

We could call the Ego a "self-forgetful" I, if the word "self-forgetful" hadn't fallen prey to a confusion between Self and I. This has happened to other beautiful words that we can no longer use to express what they literally say. *Self-serving*, for example, has come to mean Ego-serving, and we use *selfless* as if it meant Ego-less. We can be thankful for the many insights we gain as we follow the paths of language, but it will be helpful to remain aware that language sometimes reveals ambiguities and contradictions in the thinking of our ancestors from whom we inherited it.

Some compound words with *self-* have, nevertheless, remained usable, and two of them can be particularly useful to highlight a fine distinction: while the "I myself" is *self-confident*, the Ego is *self-assured*. Self-assurance presumptuously takes the Self for granted and ignores it, while self-confidence trusts the Self and gratefully relies on it. Thus, the "I myself" is self-reliant, in the sense of both relying on the Self and acting with healthy self-esteem. The Ego, in contrast, shows self-contempt—contempt for the Self and, deep down, even contempt for itself.

In contrast to the Ego, the I in "I myself" is a delightful expression of the Self. It is in communion with all others in and through the Self. This gives meaning* and orientation to my life and becomes the basis for a healthy relationship to any You I meet.

5

The You

To Live Means to Be in Relationship

Realizing that I am, from the very beginning, embedded in a network of relationships makes me ready for an important insight: the innermost essence of the word "I" is relationship.* It makes no sense to say "I" except in relation to a You. In my outer life I meet many others, each of them the one unique I to themselves, each of them another You to me. There are countless admirable little Yous in my outer world. In my inner life, however, I experience one big You—not in addition to all the little ones, but somehow including them all. Passion for a human You will prove genuine and deep, to the extent to which it embraces—in and through that human You—the Great You. Rilke's most passionate love poem addresses both dimensions of the You at once.

> *Extinguish both my eyes: I see you still;*
> *Slam shut my ears: I can still hear you talking;*
> *Without my mouth I can implore your will,*
> *And without feet, toward you I keep on walking.*
> *Break off my arms: I shall still hold you tight;*
> *My heart will yet embrace you all the same.*

15

Suppress my heart: My brain knows no deterrent;
And if at last you set my brain aflame,
I carry you still on my bloodstream's current.

That both the small and the Great You are addressed here is demonstrated by the fact that Rilke wrote these lines for Lou Andreas-Salome, the great love of his life, but shortly afterward published them with her consent in the *Book of Hours* as a prayer.

From the very start, my inner You makes it possible for me to say "I" in a meaningful way. Each outward encounter with a little You can enrich my understanding of the big inner You. This happens when I keep my eyes on the You that confronts me concretely and at the same time let that small You become transparent to the ultimate You. Only then can I make the words of E. E. Cummings my own and say with full conviction, "i am through you so i."

But how can I be so sure that my big You is more than a collective term for all my little Yous, more than just a kind of generic You? Is there really more to it? An observation that has helped me discover the "more" of my inner You is this: I experience my life as a continuous story with an unfolding plot. Don't all of us experience it that way? After all, your life is not just a series of episodes, but a story—your life story. And a story is meant to be told. The closer I feel to a friend, the more I want to share my life story. Don't you? But here we run into a surprising fact: much as we try, we can never communicate our story in its full depth to any You out there. It feels as if the deepest meaning never came across. Only our inner You, which takes part in every step of our story as it happens, seems to understand it fully. The Great You is the only one to whom we can tell our whole story. It is this You that the poet Rilke has in mind when he writes,

> *I'm always walking toward you*
> *with all my walking;*
> *for, who am I and who are you*
> *if we don't understand each other?*

From the very dawn of our consciousness, we are intuitively aware of this "walking toward," this basic orientation toward our inner You, even if we may only gradually become reflectively aware of it. And this intuitive awareness of our inner You accompanies, like background music, every one of our relationships with a You out there. At first, this will not be more than an intuition, but we can eventually reason out why this must be so: our ultimate You is at the heart of the one Great Mystery* that can be shared but never divided. The Great You is one and the same for all of us. We need to let this fact sink in. Nothing could be more important than to cultivate the relationship with our Great You.

The skeptic within you might doubt the very existence of that Great You. But there is the realist, like E. E. Cummings, who knows,

> *how should tasting touching hearing seeing*
> *breathing any—lifted from the no*
> *of all nothing—human merely being*
> *doubt unimaginable You?*[1]

Let cynics call that inner You an enlarged version of some imaginary playmate from your childhood fantasies. You know better, for you know the difference.

What you dream up does whatever you want, but the Great You often asks you to do what you don't want. In every rela-

---

[1] See "i thank You God for most this amazing," *E. E. Cummings: Complete Poems, 1904–1962* (New York: Liveright, 2016).

tionship it makes demands on you, once you begin to listen to it—wordless but powerful demands for honesty, respect, and faithfulness.

How we listen to our inner You determines the way we listen to others. That is why our relationship to the Great You is so important—not only for our own inner grounding but for the well-being of the communities to which we belong. The more attention we pay individually to our Great You, the closer we will feel to others and ready to share with them, since our own most intimate You is also our communally shared You.

The more intimately we experience mutual belonging with another person—for example, in deep friendship or mature love—the more do we notice that our partners seem to embody something beyond themselves, something that is "making powerful demands," as I said earlier.

The Great You that we encounter in the beloved person challenges and inspires us to rise to an inner stature we had not before imagined. The inner eyes of both partners in a deep relationship see the one Great You in one another. Love gives them good eyes for that reality. And all of us can train our inner eyes. The more we learn to live in the now, the more clearly do we see the lasting You in every temporary You we encounter, not only in those close to us, but in all human beings. This is crucial, for it shapes our way of treating others. It will become second nature for us to say yes to our belonging together in the Great You, simply through our way of life. That is no less than love in action.

Awareness of our shared You is usually much stronger in an I-You encounter than in what we shall call I-It encounters and explore in the next section.

Rilke, who said, "I'm always walking toward you," finds that Great You also in "things" (and in animals and plants as well).

> *I'm finding you in all these things*
> *with whom I'm close and like a brother;*
> *as a seed, you bask in the lowly ones*
> *and in the big ones you bestow yourself in a big way.*

By seeing the Great You in all things, the poet rises to a mystical height. A mystic of the Hasidic tradition in Judaism, Rabbi Yitzchak Berditchev prays ecstatically,

> *Wherever I wander—You!*
> *Whatever I ponder—You!*
> *Only You everywhere, You, always You. You, You, You.*
> *When I am gladdened—You! When I am saddened—You!*
> *Only You! Everywhere You! You, You, You.*
> *Sky is You!*
> *Earth is You!*
> *You above! You below!*
> *In every trend, at every end,*
> *Only You, everywhere You!*[2]

But isn't this blurring the distinction between people and things? No. Rather, this way of looking at things helps us to heal the violent cut by which we have separated the two worlds. We can distinguish but must not separate the world of You and the world of It.

---

[2] "Dudeleh," by Rabbi Levi Yitzchak of Berditchev, translation by Rabbi Rami Shapiro. Used by permission of the translator.

6

The It

The Great Mystery within Things

There are two perspectives under which our I can look at the world. Grammar calls them the second-person perspective and the third-person perspective. I call them, with Ferdinand Ebner and Martin Buber, the I/You perspective and the I/It perspective. They show us two different faces of our one world and account for two different ways of dealing with it.

All of us are familiar with the typical way of dealing with the world of things under the I/It perspective. We approach them with an impersonal attitude—the way science* approaches its objects and technology makes use of them. We understand ourselves as subjects who come to know things as objects through observing and analyzing them. We try to get control over them, in order to manipulate and use them for our purposes. We are used to approaching the greater part of beings with this impersonal attitude, as "mere things."

But there is also the world of people. This I/You world demands a different—a personal—approach from us, an approach in the second-person perspective. Here, we are no longer controlling and using things, but meeting and interacting with people not as objects but as subjects in their own right. We'll never come to know them by observing and analyzing them in an objective way, but only by connecting with them on a personal level. This absolutely excludes manipulation and control of people and demands instead respect for the dignity of others in their unique otherness.

The more we become aware of human dignity,* the more we'll also respect the dignity* of things. But today this happens less and less frequently. We are witnessing a twofold catastrophe. On the one hand, we are allowing the I/It world to take over our relationships with human beings. (We discuss the consequences in the next section, "The System.") On the other hand, the one world is falling apart through an extreme split between an I/You world and an I/It world because we have pushed their distinction to the point of separation. Think only of our relationship to nature. Everywhere we are "conquering nature," making it the object of manipulation and exploitation.

If you have ever hiked in the mountains, have experienced the deep silence of an ancient forest, or found that a tree in a city park can become your friend, you know that nature is more than an object. It has an additional dimension. Martin Buber speaks about that dimension. He imagines a moment when someone who is normally interested in trees merely for the shade they provide, or for the value of their wood, looks, for once, with soft eyes and with an open heart: "As I contemplate the tree I am drawn into a relation, and the tree ceases to be an It.... It confronts me bodily and has to deal with me as I must deal with it—only differently. One should not try to dilute what it means to be related: relation is reciprocity. Does the tree then have consciousness, similar to our own? I have no experience of that.... What I encounter is neither the soul of a tree nor a dryad (a tree sprite), but the tree itself."[1]

---

[1] Martin Buber, *I and Thou*, trans. Walter Kaufmann (New York: Scribner, 1970), 57–58.

How can that happen? What is going on at that moment? Have I simply projected my own awareness on that tree and so personified it? But, if you try it, it feels rather as if the initiative were coming from the side of the tree, not as in the encounter with a human You—but, well, as in a genuine encounter with a Tree-You. "Does the tree have consciousness, similar to our own?" Buber asks and modestly answers, "I have no experience of that." What matters for me is not what the tree experiences but what I do: I experience being drowned into a relationship in which more is included than this single tree, just as in the encounter with a human being more is included than this single You. What I ultimately encounter in any You, I can also encounter in any tree: Mystery. This happens, as Buber says, "through decision and grace." Both are necessary: I must decide to open my heart wide for this experience and receive it as a gift. "All is grace," said St. Augustine, all is Life's gift. And Life is the story of our adventurous encounters with that "Secret," of which, so far, we only know from Robert Frost that it "sits in the middle and knows," while "we dance in a ring and suppose." Draw out the line of any relationship into infinity and it will lead to that "Secret"—the Mystery, which we encounter in and through all that exists.

Encounters like Buber's with the tree do, in fact, occur quite frequently between humans and their dogs, horses, or cats. They can also occur with other animals and even with your plants as you water them on your windowsill and nurse a struggling one back to health. When this change of attitude happens in our heart, a broken bond is reestablished. The distinction* between the I/You and the I/It worlds is left intact, but the violent separation* between the two worlds is healed. In the unbroken world in which we can live from now on, the two perspectives overlap and gradually shade into one another. Of course, we must not expect to be able to maintain a pure I/You attitude uninterruptedly, in fact, not even in our relationships with other human beings. But we can strive to renew that attitude again and again, and so contribute to healing the cancerous spread of the I/It attitude in our society. This needs to happen if we are to save our environment and ourselves.

But existence still is enchanted; in hundreds of places it still is beginning. The playing of flawless forces that no one can touch, but who kneels and admires.

Words are still tenderly fading into what cannot be said ... And music, ever anew, is building from quivering stones in unusable space its celestial house.

(Rilke)

At the core of its existence, the natural world is still healthy, whole, and holy. It has power to heal not only itself, but us. Although we are exterminating literally hundreds of species daily, and irreparably destroying entire ecosystems, Life retains its mysterious power. Life may wipe out our own species if we do not make a complete turnaround. We need not—we cannot—reenchant the world. It has always been enchanted. We only need to open our eyes and hearts and rediscover the right relationship to its Mystery. What we need to relearn is to "kneel and admire" in reverence* and amazement. What drives us in the opposite direction is "The System."

7

"The System"

It-Ness as a Deadly Force

Not only do we systematically destroy our environment, but more and more we are treating people as objects—controlling, manipulating, using, and exploiting them, in contempt of human dignity. This means that the I/You world is rapidly losing power in our society and is dissolving, while the I/It world is taking over in all areas.

Aldous Huxley satirized that kind of society in his 1932 *Brave New World*. In that novel, human dignity is totally ignored by the dominant society, called the World State. Its highest values are cold intellect, discipline, and efficiency. In order to impress these values on children as early as possible, they are produced in a hatchery through selective cloning, and brought up in a conditioning center, designed to eliminate individuality, emotions, and any warm personal relations. The novel's only character who gets disgusted at being a cog in this perverse mechanism hangs himself in the end for the shame of having been complicit with a society designed to function like a machine. *Brave New World* describes the worst-case scenario of a takeover by the I/It world, something we ourselves are witnessing today on a vast scale, although, thank goodness, we have no hatchery but still have loving mothers, the hope of our future.

But what is the power behind that takeover? It is the life-destroying force colloquially called "The System." Countless young teachers, medical students, and political candidates with high ideals know the power of "The System" all too well. They have to face it at every turn. In a daily grind, they struggle to defend their enthusiasm and their ideals against that powerful but evasive and hard-to-define force. But let's be careful: we must not identify "The System" with the educational, medical, political, or any other system as such. Each of those systems can be life-enhancing when it functions well. It becomes life-destroying only when "The System" gains power over it and makes it dysfunctional. Isn't it amazing how little attention we pay to that distinction? By doing so, we are, in fact, confusing the patient with the disease—a sick system with "*The* System." We have to take great care to disentangle that confusion, for it can seriously distort our understanding and misguide our actions—making us blame and attack a particular sick system instead of "The System" that makes it sick.

We have to carefully distinguish between two different meanings of the word. *System* in the general sense of the term simply means a "setup"—it is the literal translation of the Greek *sustēma*—the internal arrangement of something with different parts or interacting functions. In this sense, a system may have positive or negative effects; there is no value judgment attached to that term. But "*The* System," in our special sense, always means a setup with negative effects. Urban Dictionary defines it as "something you shouldn't trust," and "Never trust 'The System'!" is indeed a phrase we often hear someone use in exasperation. If we fail to distinguish between these two meanings of "system," we can easily slide into the mistake of automatically distrusting, say,

the political or educational system, instead of facing our responsibility* to free them from the power of "The System." But what
precisely is it, and what makes it so powerful?

By calling it a system, we imply that it is a specific organizing principle. But since "The System" can influence many other
systems for the worse, it must be a principle that changes the way
in which other systems operate. And what does that change consist of? A close look shows us the answer: wherever The System
is taking over, I/You relationships are systematically turned into
the coldest I/It relationships—people are being used and abused
as things, and all the environment is thought of as mere things.

We may conceive of The System as a set of rules or commands
that can infiltrate other systems and begin to convert the relationships within them from personal into impersonal ones. That is
what happened when society was turned into the World State
in Huxley's *Brave New World*: The System eventually eliminated
every expression of mutual belonging and of mutual appreciation,
in public and in private life. That's how it functions. But how did
this monstrosity originate?

Imagine giving the doorman a smile as you hurry past him in
the morning. You show yourself grateful that he's doing his job,
rain or shine. Smiles are contagious. He smiles back and might
smile at others who go past him that day. By evening, a ripple
of your smile might have reached not only all who passed that
doorman, but all whom they, in turn, passed, and so on and on.
It might even have circled all the way back to you—improving in
its path, if ever so slightly, the social climate of the whole neigh-
borhood and beyond. But now imagine that one morning you
simply rush past the doorman. It faintly crosses your mind that
he might hope for a smile, but today you simply don't care. The
good man feels only a ripple of disappointment, but by evening
he will have passed on your small lack of kindness to a multitude
of other people, and this will continue making the social climate

colder. This time, there wasn't even something passed on, like your smile had been. Just something that belonged there—an act of human warmth and kindness—was left missing. Instead, there was a gaping hole, as it were, that produced hole after hole. The System consists of a pattern of holes in spots where something essential is lacking. Over time, this lack of love—for that's what the holes ultimately are—keeps expanding in a self-perpetuating vicious circle, invading, like a cold front, other systems and changing their climate.

In growing numbers, people in our society feel irrelevant. This not only affects them personally by making them feel depressed, but it also affects society as a whole, since people who feel irrelevant lack the drive and confidence to contribute to the necessary changes and to tackle the great challenges of our time. It is amazing how much power a smile or simply an acknowledging look at someone has, to make that person feel relevant and empowered. We need to become aware of this power. Each one of us has it, and the world is urgently waiting for us to make use of it.

But what is it that keeps The System going for ages and ages? Why doesn't it run out of steam? Well, because there never was any steam in it in the first place. We called it "a pattern of holes" through which the steam escapes, so to say—the steam that powers kind human interaction. Wherever there would be a Yes to belonging, The System has a hole—a No.

But if it is ultimately nothing that is spreading there, what gives The System its tremendous impact? And if it is a completely impersonal entity, how can it exert such force on people and personal relationships? Looking for an example, I was trying to find something that causes great damage and yet is a mere lack. What came to mind was a missing screw in an airplane engine. This tiny lack could cause a gigantic disaster. Overlooking one little screw may seem a minor matter, yet minor matters matter all the more for being so easily overlooked.

How easy it is, through lack of mindfulness, to miss an opportunity for expressing and spreading the warmth of human relationships. Every encounter implies a decision: will I answer yes or no to Life's invitation to let the one I meet feel accepted and valued? If our yes is lacking, this lack, though it may concern only a small matter, is our personal contribution to the impersonal violence* of The System that can lead a whole society into disaster.

Unfortunately, it is all too easy to slide into ruts in the roads of The System. Mottos sometimes express such ruts that make careless drivers skid. When corrupt behavior becomes an expectation, we may find ourselves repeating, thoughtlessly and with a cynical grin, a cliché such as, "Trust is good, but control is better." We do not even notice the devastating effect such a principle has on the interaction between people.

And lack of trust, no matter how small in its beginning, is not the only way in which we feed The System with personal energy. There are always some who—shortsightedly—see some advantage in treating people like things, using and exploiting them for one's own advancement. Thereby they are giving The System a foothold in politics, in the economy, or in whatever other system they are wielding power, and from that starting point The System can spread. I called their behavior shortsighted, since, in the long run, a world without mutual trust and caring love turns self-destructive.

And yet, in addition to those few profiteers, countless others still stand only to lose by The System and are nevertheless supporting it—by hiding behind it. It gives them something to blame, and they use it as a scapegoat, instead of taking a stand against it. Aren't we all tempted, now and then, through laziness to fall into that trap?

What does it mean to take a stance against The System? It means recognizing its manifestations in public life and taking public action—petitions, demonstrations, strikes, boycotts. We want to keep in mind, however, that we are not attacking this or that system as such, but its corruption by The System. We are not attacking the rich or powerful, but their corrupt actions. Those who are wielding power within The System are actually at the same time its victims. Even the hearts of those who profit most from it are longing—whether or not they are aware of it—to be liberated from their love of power by the power of love.

This points to the second way of taking action against The System—the less visible, but equally important one: multiplying acts of personal kindness. Any system corrupted by The System is full of holes, gaps, where personal relationships have been damaged. There are—on every level of society, in every profession, and certainly among the unemployed and most neglected among us—innumerable hidden heroes in the struggle against The System. All these men and women daily do the most important thing in life: they do their tasks, no matter how humdrum, and show kindness to everyone they meet—make them aware that someone cares.

The origin of caring is motherlove. Passing on the love and care we received at birth takes a lifetime. The strongest counter-force to The System is mothers. And—men or women—we are capable of mothering in many ways.

However, motherly caring and friendly smiles alone cannot do the trick. Resistance to The System requires a tactically targeted action plan. Developing a smart, well-thought-out, and hard-nosed strategy for dismantling it is our urgent task. In this effort, each one of us has a part to play and is responsible for finding out what our part is. Whatever our tactical role may be, it will not replace, however, caring smiles and friendliness toward strangers. Even though friendliness must never become a strategy, any strategy must be able to smile in a friendly way in order to achieve its goal.

It is most typical for The System that it cannot smile and does not care. It is a totally impersonal power, although it works as if it were driven by some super-powerful monomaniac. In fact, it is the manifestation of utter impersonality—the epitome of It-ness as a deadly force. Its ideology has one goal: a world purged of all ties of personal belonging and of all unique personal creativity. In order to achieve this goal, it will suppress and destroy human dignity in all its manifestations. Put positively and succinctly, taking a stance against The System ultimately means standing up for human dignity.

But how can we have reverence for human dignity unless we stand in awe* before the Mystery? Human dignity is rooted in Mystery.

8

Mystery

Understanding the Incomprehensible

Our English word "mystery" comes from a Greek verb with the root meaning of "shutting"—closing your eyes or shutting up. (The word "mute" comes from the same linguistic root.) Mystery commands silence, since it is precisely that which cannot be put into words. By definition, we cannot possibly *comprehend* mystery intellectually, cannot grasp it by means of logical terms, and yet we can *understand* it.

The distinction between comprehension* and understanding* is a most important one. We may not have reflected on the difference between these two forms of coming to know something, but we are familiar with it—from our experience with music. No intellectual analysis can ever hope to grasp music in its essence. Yet we can deeply understand music, in moments when we are being moved by it. This understanding implies more than mere emotions. It is an insight deeper even than intellectual comprehension. T. S. Eliot has such moments in mind when he speaks in *The Four Quartets* of "music heard so deeply / that it is not heard at all, but you are the music / while the music lasts." Our "being

31

moved" implies that music must "do something" to us before we can understand it.

Thus, mystery is not a vague and mystifying term. We can clearly spell out what we mean by it. Mystery is a power that we can never comprehend but understand through its impact on us. As it is with music, so with mystery. We cannot understand it unless we open ourselves to what it does to us. "What we can grasp gives us knowledge, but that which 'grabs us' gives us wisdom," says the great medieval mystic Bernard of Clairvaux.

A mystic,* as the word suggests, is someone who lives in touch with Mystery. In this respect, all of us are mystics. In our Peak Experiences,* we become aware of that fact, but whether we are aware of this or not, we are at all times immersed in Mystery. Mystery is the power that empowers nature. It is in us and all around us, present and active in all there is.

When I ask myself, "Who am I?" it does not take long for me to reach a point where I no longer *comprehend* myself, but I do *understand* who I am: I am rooted in Mystery. I find this to be true also of everything around me: when I inquire into anything deeply and long enough, my quest leads into Mystery.

There are three existential questions that we human beings seem to be programmed, as it were, to ask, sooner or later: Why? What? and How? All three lead into Mystery.

Asking "Why?" about anything may yield a few satisfactory reasons, but if we submit these superficial answers in their turn to further why?, this will soon lead us to ask an even more basic question: "Why is there anything at all, rather than nothing?" Children sometimes ask this, since they are natural philosophers, before school teaches them not to ask such "stupid questions." And what is the answer? Only silence—a special kind of silence, the silence of awe whenever Mystery touches us. The question "Why?" can lead us to understand Mystery as the *nothing* of unlimited possibility that brings forth everything there is.

If, instead, we look now at *every*thing around us and ask "What?"—what is this and this and this?—we won't have to go very far beyond the grid of classification within which we give things a name and a place before we intuit something that challenges every effort to put it into words. Gerard Manley Hopkins spoke of this essence of things as their inner being, which they "deal out" or radiate simply by being themselves, by "selving," as he calls it.

> *Each mortal thing does one thing and the same:*
> *Deals out that being indoors each one dwells;*
> *Selves—goes itself; myself it speaks and spells,*
> *Crying Whát I dó is me: for that I came.*

> *("As Kingfishers Catch Fire")*

By *selving*, things, as it were, spell their own name, not waiting for us to give them one. They speak that name, they are even *crying* it out, but we cannot grasp that word—that name; only if we listen deeply enough to be grasped by it do we understand it. That's how the question "What?" leads us into Mystery.

This is also where the third of our existential questions leads us. By "How?" we ask for the dynamic aspect of things, for their workings—from subatomic particles to atoms and molecules, and on to planets, stars, galaxies, and super galaxies. *How* are they "doing their thing"? We know that the whole universe is driven by energy, and we can even formulate some "laws" according to which energy works, but what energy is in itself no one knows. Living beings, too, are powered by energy, but we can't know through outside observation how they experience being alive. Since we ourselves are living beings, however, we can ask, how do *we* experience the dynamic drive of our aliveness? "Through living," is the answer. Although we understand quite well what that means, we cannot grasp it logically. Life is bigger than logic.

And so, the question How? also leads us ultimately into Mystery.

Why, what, and *how*: all three of them will, if we ask persistently enough, make us aware of Mystery, but under three different aspects. *Why* asks for the roots, the origin of everything, and so leads us down into the unspeakable ground of being—Mystery as silence. *What* asks for the innermost essence of things and ends up listening to the name that each thing "speaks and spells" in *selving*—Mystery as word. *How* asks for the dynamic force driving things from within, but that force is beyond our grasp; we can understand it only by experiencing the driving force within ourselves, only by living life—Mystery as understanding-by-doing. If you stay alert, you will encounter these three doorways into Mystery, in ever-new variations.

Silence,* word,* and understanding-by-doing*: all three are necessary for finding meaning. Any genuine word must come out of silence and be welcomed in silence; otherwise, it is mere chit-chat. If we listen deeply to that word, it will take hold of us and move us to respond. If we respond by doing what the word sends us to do, we will understand. This deep listening is obedience* in the full sense of the word. And through our obedient doing, the word that has taken hold of us will carry us back into the silence out of which it came. Do you recognize this movement as a circle dance? Indeed, it is another way of understanding what "it's all about." After all, isn't the goal of our search for orientation the discovery of meaning?

9

Life

The Process of Encountering Mystery

It is through living life that we encounter mystery and thus find meaning. And by living life fully we inevitably encounter mystery. If we have understood this connection and keep it in mind, we won't ever use the word "life" without implying at the same time "mystery."

Full aliveness implies both: learning to understand, affirm, and celebrate the life of nature and living our personal life in harmony with it. We shall consider these two separately but must remember that they belong inseparably together.

There is a special word for learning to understand the life processes of nature and applying their principles to human communities: ecoliteracy.* Fritjof Capra coined that term and explains that nature works according to three basic principles: networking, recycling, and reliance on solar energy. As he puts it, "Life's basic pattern of organization is the network; matter cycles continually through the web of life; all ecological cycles are sustained by . . . energy from the sun."[1]

---

[1] Fritjof Capra, *The Web of Life: A New Scientific Understanding of Living Systems* (New York: Anchor Books, 1997), 7.

To become ecoliterate is the most urgent task for the human family today; our survival as a species depends on modeling our communities, social institutions, and technologies on nature. Training in ecoliteracy must involve our intellect, but also our will and our emotions. It demands that we become well informed about the natural world and the principles by which it operates. But information must lead to action, and this can only come about through our willing and determined commitment. Closing the gap between knowing and acting is the crucial step—and the most difficult one. The truism is well put: *Life does not reward you for what you know, but for what you do.* Life demands our full and active attunement to its principles of operation—the alternative is self-destruction. The chilling last lines of William Empson's poem "Missing Dates" point to nature's built-in sanctions against poisoning our environment: "Slowly the poison the whole blood stream fills. / The waste remains, the waste remains and kills."

But when we do act responsibly, nature rewards us with life in abundance. The joy of children learning ecoliteracy by tending their own school garden—smelling rich soil, putting seeds into the ground, watching them sprout and grow, and eventually munching radishes they themselves planted—this joy adds to intellectual input and training of the will: the third, the emotional aspect of ecoliteracy. And this joy could characterize a whole society. Earth has all it takes to be a garden overflowing with joyful Life for those well informed about nature's basic principles and willing to put them into practice.

What we have seen here concerning life on the largest scale also concerns our individual lives quite intimately, for we are embedded in countless networks of nature and society, and our well-being depends on their functioning. Hence, in our effort at orientation, we want to look at the keyword life also on the small scale and ask, what is my personal life all about? Well, what is that dynamic process that we call "my life" all about? We experience it as a development.*

That word "development" has three aspects, each of them relevant for the process of our personal lives. The first meaning of development suggests the process of bodily changes that we share with all other living beings. But development can also mean gradual enrichment, as when we develop our vocabulary or our network of friends on, say, Facebook or Instagram. And the dictionary gives us a third meaning of development as "the process of treating photographic film with chemicals to make a visible image." This provides a fitting metaphor for finding our genuine self-image.

In order to mature to full sweetness, we humans need to experience, as wide awake as possible, the process of the growing, blossoming, fruit-bearing, and decline of our bodies, with all the emotions of delight and sadness evoked by the different stages. We also need to develop a treasure of relationships by expanding and strengthening our connections to all the different networks that enrich our life-experience. And we need to develop, with the skill of a master photographer, our self-image, from an originally confused one to an ever clearer one. This is the great task of "Know thyself!"

Each of these three ways of our development throughout our life leads deep into mystery. At each step of our natural development, our growing and thriving and dying (for we die many times in a lifetime), we experience mystery as the unfathomable ground of our aliveness. And our treasure of relationships does not develop by analyzing them but by allowing them to touch us deeply. That touch that gives us understanding where we cannot comprehend is, as we have come to see, the touch of mystery. Finally, we develop our authentic self-image by allowing mystery to shine through both highlights and shadows of who we are. Do we not get a sense of mystery when we look long and with compassion at ourselves in a mirror? (Trying this out is a worth-while spiritual exercise.)

Thus, by looking at life at both the all-embracing and the individual scales, we have found mystery to be an ever-recurring keyword for our orientation. Life in nature makes us encounter mystery, and so does life experienced in our personal lives. We might now briefly explore how the two, life and mystery, are connected by a third keyword: blessing.

10

Blessing

Bloodstream of the Universe

The word "blessing" suggests something blissful, as when we speak of "a blessing in disguise." The ultimate blessing is life in all its fullness.

A rabbi once gave me a deep and most beautiful image of blessing. (I have forgotten his name, and I sincerely apologize for that.) In the Holy Land, as in other places where rain is scarce, water is the most perfect symbol for blessing. Thus, the River Jordan, cascading down from the Lebanon Mountains, brings blessing wherever it flows. It fills Lake Tiberias, the Sea of Galilee, with an abundance of fish and makes the gardens and orchards on its shores a paradise of fruitfulness. Flowing through the lake and on, the river descends into the deepest depression on Earth, the Dead Sea. True to its name, the Dead Sea looks completely dead. Its shores are a waste of rocks, encrusted with salt. Its water, many times saltier than ocean water, is empty of fish, and a diver swallowing some of it would at once choke to death. But isn't this the same water that brought abundant life to the Sea of Galilee? "Yes," answers the rabbi, "but here is the significant difference:

the Sea of Galilee receives the waters of the Jordan and lets them flow out again. The Dead Sea has no outflow, so the water of life gets stagnant in it and spells death. This is exactly what happens to a blessing we receive if we don't pass it on."

The word "blessing" comes from the same linguistic root as "blood." Blessing is the bloodstream of the universe. It needs to be kept circulating. By living our personal life to the full, we tap into the life of nature as a whole, and so into mystery, the silent source of all blessing. Through paying full attention to our physical life throughout its seasons, we become aware of taking part in the great web of life and its unfolding, the unveiling of mystery as a story, a word. Through participating in the networks that enrich our life, we experience the continuous circulation of natural and cultural energy, which is the very circulation of blessing through the universe, and, deeply understood, the flow of mystery as Word,* through understanding-by-doing,* into silence.* And just as all ecological cycles are sustained by the energy of the sun, so the source of all blessing in our personal life is ultimately our dynamic relationship with mystery as the great You at our innermost center of silence.

11

God

Mystery as Our Great You

There are some serious problems with the G-word. Many people are allergic to it; they find it hard to unlearn the misleading notion of God they have been taught and can't forget the repugnant things done through our history "in the name of God." They don't want to hear that word ever again. (If you happen to be one of them, I beg you to continue reading, as if you had never heard that word before.) For society as a whole, it can become dangerously divisive that different groups hold on tenaciously to their respective notions of God and fight against all who have a different notion. And yet, God can instead become a uniting concept and thus an important keyword for our orientation, if we explore its authentic meaning. That is what we try to do here.

The word "God" originated early in the history of our language and goes back to the Indo-European root *gheu*, with the meaning of "calling." God was originally understood to mean "the called-upon," but perhaps also "that which is calling us." In any case, the notion of calling suggests the reciprocity of an I/You relationship. At the same time, however, the original gender of the word was neither male nor female, but neuter, thus avoiding the danger of projecting too human an image on God. There are still native societies in our time whose religion resembles that of prehistoric cultures. Anthropological fieldwork shows that they often worship personifications of natural forces, like storms or lightning, and yet above and beyond these "gods," they acknowledge a Great Spirit or Great Mystery, a highest Power, of which they speak in less anthropomorphic images. For example, Chief Luther Standing Bear said, "From Wakan Tanka, the Great Spirit, there came a great unifying life force that flowed in and through all things."[1] Black Elk spoke of our relationship to that Force and of the great inner "peace ... which comes within the souls of people when they realize their relationship, their oneness with the universe and all its powers." But he went a step further and spoke of that relationship as a personal one, and of the peace that people experience "when they realize that at the center of the universe dwells the Great Spirit, and that its center is really everywhere, it is within each of us."[2] We could describe that decisive step in terms we have been using and call it the momentous discovery that even though "we live and move and have our being" (Acts 17:28) in mystery, it is also our Big You.

God means the ultimate Mystery under the aspect of our I/You relationship with it.

The term "God" is not a name,* but we might call it a code word that refers to the nameless, incomprehensible power that cannot be conceptualized, and to which our human awareness stands in its deepest personal relationship. But in the course of history, this personal relationship has often been emphasized

---

[1] See *The Wisdom of Native Americans*, ed. Kent Nerburn (Novato, CA: New World Library, 1999), 15.

[2] See John G. Neihardt, *Black Elk Speaks: Being the Life Story of a Holy Man of the Oglala Sioux* (Lincoln: University of Nebraska Press, 2008).

much more than the fact that "God" refers to the incomprehensible mystery. When this happens, the word is easily misunderstood as the name of a supreme deity, of whom we cannot help speaking in mythical images. Rilke says of this process, "Our image-fashioning hands obscure you, whenever our hearts behold you unveiled."

Clinging to images or names for God remains a constant danger. We are free to enjoy those poetic names and images, as long as we do not take them literally. At the moment we do so and cling to them, they threaten our personal relationship with God that can only thrive if we allow the unimaginable to take hold of us again and again. Moreover, putting too much emphasis on names and images of God quickly leads to disagreement between us, because we overlook too easily the fact that they all point to one and the same great unifying life force.

In that Mystery of Life, in that great unifying life force, all of us "live and move and have our being," not merely like fish in the ocean, but like drops of its very water—yet we are not lost in that "ocean" as in an impersonal soup. We are immersed in it, but at the same time in a personal relationship with it, as the great You to our little I. Buddhist teachers often use the image of ocean and wave to speak of our coming forth from Mystery at our birth and returning to it in death.* One day I asked Eido Shimano Roshi, one of my Zen teachers, about a problem with that image. Now, as waves, we have a sense of personhood that has many positive aspects, such as self-awareness, responsibility, and compassion. Are we to lose all this and go back into an impersonal ocean? "Where could the wave have it from, if the ocean didn't have it?" he asked in reply.

God stands for the personal aspect of mystery, as we've said, but that doesn't mean that God is "a person," in the sense in which we use this word in everyday language. God, Mystery, "the ocean" must have all the perfections of personhood, but none of the limitations of that concept. For instance, a person cannot, at the same time, be a different person. But God is the You we encounter in and through every person we meet, in ever-new variations. In fact, we encounter God in everything there is and in the innermost depth of *ourselves*. In this sense, the Christian monk and mystic Thomas Merton can say, "God is not someone else."

Here we find ourselves again face-to-face with the most mysterious aspect of Mystery: it constitutes our innermost Self, and yet we stand in relationship to it as the altogether Other. Our innermost Self participates in Mystery—that is to say, in God; and yet, God is also our Great You.

The idea that we should "love God more than this or that person" is altogether misconceived. Any love is ultimately love of God. No love can be in competition with love of God; it is merely a different expression of it. The person we love may loom so large in the foreground that we do not explicitly think of our love as aiming at God, but the deeper, the more passionate *any* love, the more truly it is love of God.

Our most exciting, most passionate personal relationship is with God—not in competition with any other relationship, but in and through *all* relationships in life. As children, we love to play "Catch me, Daddy!" and throw ourselves into the outstretched arms of someone in whom we have limitless trust—and by that we mean implicitly Life, Mystery, God. We can reenact that game with abandon and devotion, whenever we act with trust in Life. All the amazement during our most thrilling explorations of nature and culture, all the deepest relationships in our life, point ultimately toward God. Whatever we experience, there is always more to it: the "more" of Mystery in its infinite expanse. That's why Dorothée Sölle speaks of God as "The More"—The More and Ever More, we might say. And the poet Rilke prays, "It is only in doing, that we can understand You." The things in life that we do with our most genuine enthusiasm are ultimately empowered by Mystery, and are—if only we wake up to it—ways of coming to know God. *Enthusiastic* is, in fact, originally a Greek word meaning "inspired by God within."

When we use the word "God" in this sense, it refers to our deepest I/You relationship. And that is an awareness we can neglect or suppress, but never deny. Martin Buber showed that this I/You relationship is universal and basic to human consciousness. Justin Richards, famous primarily as a skateboarder, writes, "Buber's God does not require belief,* belief belongs to the world of objects, and no orientation toward an object can substitute for the absolute relation to an eternal You. The atheist who enters into authentic relations with his fellow humans has more to do with God than the believer who remains forever firmly in the I/It world."[3] The atheist may not want to name as God "The More and Ever More" within every authentic relation. Let's not insist on words—least of all on the G-word. Words often divide. The experience of encountering in every human relationship a surpassing You unites us. And an experience it is, not a projection.

Projections, wrongly called God, are all too widespread. They are of two basic types: an outsize cosmic Santa Claus and a Super-Policeman of the same colossal dimensions. These two can easily fuse into one another, since Santa "*knows* if you've been *bad* or *good.* *So* be *good* for *goodness' sake!*"

A child's developing relation to the big You can easily get misled and distorted by one or both of these projections. If the Super-Policeman replaces the big You, the child may have to struggle ever after with guilt feelings and fear. And if the idol of a wish-fulfilling Santa usurps the place of the big You in people's

---

[3] Justin Richards, "You and I, I and It: Martin Buber's I and Thou," *Epoche Philosophy Monthly*, September 2017, https://epochemagazine. org/06/you-and-i-i-and-it-martin-bubers-i-and-thou/#:~:text=Buber's percent20God percent20does percent20not percent20require,relation percent20to percent20an percent20eternal percent20You.

imagination, a bitter experience will sooner or later make them cry out, "How can a loving God do such things?" In either case, atheism will be the most likely consequence of discovering that "*there ain't no Santa Claus.*" The tears that many adults still remember shedding when they made that discovery bear witness to an existential disappointment—the death of God—because Santa could no longer be distinguished from the big You. To forestall such heartache is a formidable task for parents. In order to accomplish this task, they will, first of all, have to cultivate awe and reverence for mystery in their own life. Only then will they be able to stand up to the pressure of society and somehow convey to their children this attitude toward Ultimate Reality. It is something quite different from the playful, make-believe attitude toward Santa Claus. Children have an inborn sense of the difference between these two. If it is handled as loving make-believe, Santa Claus's coming to town and all that goes with it present no danger to a child's development. On the contrary, it can become a valuable stimulus for the little one's flowering imagination.

How can we tell the all-important difference between God as Ultimate Reality and "God" as mere projection? Anything that can become an "it" cannot be God, who is our ultimate You. "By its very nature, the eternal You cannot become an It," wrote Martin Buber. And we quoted Justin Richard above: "No orientation toward an object can substitute for the absolute relation to an eternal You." Eido Roshi expressed the same profound insight: "You cannot speak about God 'in profile,' but only to God, face to face." He was not speaking as a Buddhist, nor from the point of view of any other religion but was drawing on the wisdom of a religiousness shared by all human hearts. The two keywords in the previous sentence—religiousness* and religion*—and are so important for spiritual orientation that we need to devote a special section to each of them.

12

Religiousness

Our Sense for the Sacred

In 1932, in "My Credo," Albert Einstein wrote: "The most beautiful and deepest experience [we humans] can have is the sense of the mysterious." He was obviously speaking of what we have called mystery.* "It is the underlying principle of religion as well as all serious endeavor in art and science." Einstein sees not only *religion* but *all serious endeavor in art and science*—all weighty human undertaking—as ways of exploring Mystery, much like Christopher Fry in powerful lines from his verse play, *A Sleep of Prisoners*:

> *The enterprise*
> *Is exploration into God.*

Since this expresses the essence of the human venture, Einstein sees the failure to rise to this task as blindness, if not as failure to come alive altogether: a person "who never had this experience seems to me, if not dead, then at least blind." Einstein characterizes his own religiousness thus: "To sense that behind anything that can be experienced there is a something that our mind cannot grasp [i.e., Mystery] and whose beauty and sublimity reaches us only indirectly and as a feeble reflection, this is

47

religiousness. In this sense, I am religious."[1] He had distanced
himself from his Jewish religion in its "prescientific" understanding, but clearly stated, "I am religious," in the sense of being
committed to religiousness, as "the underlying principle of religion"—an excellent definition of it.

This commitment, as Einstein knew, is a commitment to being
human. That we have to interact with unfathomable, inexhaustible, unstoppable life is the basic fact of our human existence. The
human mind is by its very nature bent on diving into mystery, on
understanding it, and on guiding our actions based on that understanding. This is how our religiousness, our lifelong interaction
with Ultimate Reality, flowers and bears fruit.

Any encounter with mystery—most typically in a peak experience, but potentially at any moment in daily life—spontaneously
triggers awe, the primal religious feeling. Awe is a paradoxical
mixture of irresistible attraction and deeply stirring dread. We can
observe both these aspects by watching a small child being awed
by the waves at the beach: the child is enticed and at the same
time scared by this encounter. Every time a wave draws back, the
toddler crows with delight and tries to chase after it, but when the
wave starts to return, the little one screams in frightened excite-
ment and scrambles toward the shore.

Rudolf Otto made a thorough study of the human attitude
toward the holy.* He speaks of the two emotions that the sacred
triggers in us, as "*fascinans*" and "*tremendum*"—as what fasci-
nates us and what makes us tremble. The intimate relationship
with mystery as our innermost You attracts us with overpowering
fascination; the vertiginous abyss of mystery makes us draw back,
trembling; and the amazing mix of these two emotions brims over

---

[1] Quoted by Robert K. Bolger and Robert C. Coburn, *Religious Language, Meaning, and Use: The God Who Is Not There* (New York: Blooms-
bury Academic, 2021), 9.

and expresses itself as the reverent awe at the core of religiousness. This happens in peak moments, but it can indeed also characterize our everyday life. As long as our hearts retain a childlike sensitivity for the holy, any interaction with people, animals, plants, and even with inanimate things gains a sacred dimension. If you have had the opportunity to live for a while in a culture that never lost its sense of the sacredness of everything, you will remember the rich life of its people—often in spite of abject poverty—compared with the frequent emptiness of life in a typical affluent society devoid of any sense of mystery. Religiousness is our innate sense for this.

13

Religions

Different Languages for the Unspeakable

The different religions are so many expressions of the one religiousness. In this sense, Raimon Panikkar compared religiousness with our human ability to speak, and the religions of the world with the different languages in which that ability expresses itself. *Ability* to speak is not sufficient for actual communication; it needs to express itself in a particular language. In the same way, religiousness needs a particular religion to express itself—many different languages, in fact, to express its fullness. What treasures would we lose if there were only one language—only one religion!

We may also find a different image useful, comparing religiousness with a huge underground reservoir from which a multitude of wells draw water. At different moments in history, the founder of a religious tradition comes along and digs a new well. The wells may differ widely from each other, according to the personality of the one who built it, the given circumstances of the place and its people, and their needs at that historic moment. We can enjoy the resulting differences between the wells if we remember that from each of them flows one and the same water.

If we grow up within a particular religious tradition, its teachings, its moral code, and its rituals will reveal their deeper meaning to us, only to the extent to which they resonate with our personal awareness of Mystery—our religiousness—and become its genuine expression. Any religion can become the language in which we speak of the unspeakable Mystery that our religiousness intuits. It is more difficult, however, later in life to learn a new language. Learning the grammar of a religious tradition by growing up in it is a rich endowment for the rest of one's life. Hence, it can be very painful to become aware that you can no longer authentically express your religiousness in the language of the religion in which you grew up. Leaving behind forms in which you used to practice your religiousness, and practicing it now in new and different forms, may appear—to others and even to yourself—as betrayal. Yet it is more likely to prove your faithfulness to the same deep content that both the old and the new forms aim to express and your brave dedication to finding your authentic expression.

You might ask, does religiousness *need to* express itself in religion? Experience shows that it does so, inevitably. Not necessarily, of course, in this or that particular religion, but inevitably in a set of phenomena—a doctrine, a moral code, and rituals—developed by the different religions in ever-new variations. It would seem relatively easy for people who can no longer identify with one particular religion to pick and choose elements from different ones. The difficulty is that religiousness is also the basis for our sense of community, and all the elements of religion are *communal* expressions of religiousness. In fact, an essential aspect of religiousness—the central aspect—is relatedness. "*Private* religiousness" is therefore a contradiction in terms. The abstract concept of relatedness becomes concrete, belonging to a community when religiousness expresses itself in religion.

Today, there are two options for practicing religion in community with others. First, joining the community of an existing religious tradition. But many seekers today just can't find one that resonates in their heart, and jumping from one to another is a lonely journey. The advice that Swami Satchidananda gave in this case was, "Keep digging. There is a better chance of hitting water when you keep digging in one place than when you dig one shallow hole after the other."

A second option is joining a community that creates its own eclectic religion by adopting teachings, morals, and rituals from a variety of sources and inventing new ones. Individual members may stand closer to this or that existing tradition and lead the whole community in appreciating the teachings of that tradition, in understanding its morals, and in celebrating its rituals. There are now communities in which all fast during Ramadan, share Seder meals, build a sweat lodge, and celebrate Christmas together, in addition to rituals invented on the spot.

Let us now look at the process by which religiousness inevitably becomes religion. Take an example you might know from experience. Remember one of your peak moments. Whatever the external circumstances, Mystery "gripped" you, and for a timeless, mystical Now, you experienced being all one within yourself, and one with all. While this experience lasts, you do not think, or wish, or feel—or rather, thinking, wishing, and feeling are indistinguishably one, within an all-embracing oneness. As soon as the experience is over, however, your intellect inevitably asks, "What was that?" and gives it a place within your mental frame of reference. This is the seed for doctrine,* the intellectual element of every religion. Not only your intellect but also your will responds to your peak experience*; it focuses on the bliss of universal belonging that you experienced a moment ago and commits itself inevitably to striving for such belonging. This "yes" to belonging is the seed for a moral code,* the ethical element of every religion. As widely as moral codes may differ, all of them say in essence: this is how one behaves toward those to whom one belongs. Finally, your emotions also respond to the peak experience you just had. Resonating with its joy, your emotions inevitably want to celebrate. And this is the seed for ritual,* the third element of every religion.

What we observed here on a small scale happens also on a large one, in the origin of any religion. It will have its source in its founder's mystical experience. This will find expression in a doctrine set within the intellectual framework of a given culture and the people to whom it is addressed—although attempting to stretch their mental frame. It will express itself in a moral code, translating the ideal of universal belonging into concrete forms that can be realized in that society. And it will call forth various forms of ritual based on the culture of that time and place. The water of that fountain may flow on and swell into a broad stream, bringing orientation through a new brand of wisdom, justice, and joy to more and more people.

Sooner or later, however, religions tend to lose their original power. One reason is that large communities can hardly avoid becoming institutions,* and all institutions have a tendency to forget the purpose* they were set up to serve; instead, they become self-serving. Another danger for religions is that they can fall under the spell of The System. When this happens, their I/You spirituality freezes into an I/It ideology: doctrine, morals, and rituals turn into dogmatism, moralism, and ritualism. What are we to do when this catastrophe befalls our own religion and the living water that once gushed forth from the fountain turns into ice? We can still thaw that ice—by the warmth of our own lifeblood. The heart of every religion is the religion of the heart, our religiousness. Personal encounter with Mystery must keep our religion alive if we, in turn, are to drink from its life-giving waters.

But if it is religiousness of our heart that ultimately matters, can we say that religions are important at all? I have two conflicting answers to this basic question. I cannot build a bridge between them. Therefore, I will, in all honesty, present them here one after the other and let readers take out of them what they find helpful.

My first answer is: religions express and thereby sustain religiousness. Their teachings, ethical guidelines, and artistic expressions provide the most effective means to remain plugged into the current of our innate sense of Mystery. This gives religion importance under three aspects.

1. Religion can give us strength to stand up against The System. Even where religious institutions themselves fall prey to The System, small networks survive within those institutions and stay vigorous in the original spirit. And even corrupted religious institutions keep life-giving water flowing into the world through their teachings, although their representatives might disregard those teachings. Thus, even the rusty pipes of religious institutions carry fresh water.

2. Religion provides a clear set of coordinates within which a child's inner life can gradually discover forms to express itself in its outer life. Children need that support, for which nothing else can substitute. They enjoy mythic stories, want clear and firm guidelines for their behavior, and enter with enthusiasm into rituals. These can be most readily supplied by one of the religious traditions, but also by eclectic religious forms that their caregivers have made their own. Of course, nothing will convince our children unless we ourselves are convinced of it.

3. Religion, whether inherited as an intact whole or pieced together eclectically according to our needs, articulates clearly what our religiousness surmises only inarticulately. It hands us no more than a map, but that map can be a valuable help in finding our orientation toward the magnetic pole of our heart's* compass—the great You, the heart of Mystery.

My second answer is triggered by the Dalai Lama's statement "Ethics is more important than religion." Maybe the religions we know have run their course and are even on their way out—largely because they divided us—and we will have to replace them by a universally valid ethics—what we've called religiousness—that unites us. A sober look at our world makes me take this possibility seriously. In this case, however, I would have to change each of the three reasons I gave for the importance of religion.

- To many of my friends and, in my saddest hours, to myself, some religions (at least), have become so infested by The System that there is no cure for them. In those cases, self-serving interests prevent their members from even thirsting for the living waters of the original message. This is not true for me personally. I stand within the Catholic Christianity that has nurtured me throughout my life, but I can see that only a dwindling number of young people find it nourishing anymore.
- While I am still convinced that religions can give much support to children, providing what they need as they grow up, religious education in practice often insists on teachings that do the opposite, inciting guilt feelings, fear, and aggression in children.
- Too often religions fall into dogmatism, moralism, and ritualism, generating a deep confusion in the hearts of their followers, diverting them from their inner sense of Mystery. And not enough people have the strength to heal these evils by the religion of the heart.

If this amounts to saying that we do not need religion but our inborn ethics will suffice, this answer leaves us with an even more difficult question: how are we to give concrete form to our inner ethics the way religions give concrete form to our religiousness? If, indeed, we are witnessing the demise of the traditional religions, who will create teachings, morals, and rituals to express universal ethics? And will one form of expression be able to serve the multitude of cultures in the world? If we define religion as a way to understand, to behave, and to celebrate the Mystery of Life, there will always be religion. The transition from hunter-gatherer cultures to agriculture triggered the first beginnings of today's great religions. Today we are witnessing a similarly dramatic transition. My whole heart goes out to the children who will have to find their way through these upheavals. For the moment, lucky are the ones who can still make the best of one of the old traditions.

Could it be that most religions as we know them are in crisis because their organizational structure is the pyramid, and the newly evolving consciousness makes it inevitable to replace the power pyramid with the network in every field of human activity? Our future, if we are to have one, will have to be in tune with nature, and nature is a network of networks. Every communal structure must be able to maintain the tension between personal independence and communal bonding—Raimon Panikkar speaks of "inter-independence" as the goal. The pyramid proved unable to achieve this goal. We will have to make every effort for the networks will succeed in this task. Maybe even the legitimate claims of any religion on its members' loyalty have necessarily a tinge of totalitarianism and therefore can hardly escape abuse. In every religion, countless faithful members have managed to navigate these dangerous waters successfully. Maybe it will always remain an inherent challenge of membership in a religion to be aware of this danger and surmount it through our personal relationship with Mystery. With regard to the future of Christianity, Karl Rahner said, "The Christian of the future will be a mystic, or he will not exist at all," and this will apply to any religion.

When we are using the map provided by one of the traditional religions and its meaning dawns on us, our heart begins to resonate with the heart of Mystery, and we want to cry out, "This is it!" This aha moment is what our spiritual journey is all about, and it is what religions are all about: the quest for meaning. We spoke already about the process of finding meaning through the three existential questions. The "why" leads us into the bottomless silence of Mystery; through "what," we come to recognize everything there is as a word that Mystery addresses to us; and "how" reaches out toward understanding Mystery by doing. Summing this up, by a formula we have used before, we can say that we find meaning by listening to the word in whatever form, so deeply that it takes hold of us, leads us to obedient action, and thus, through understanding-by-doing, brings us into a new level of the silence out of which it came.

In the various expressions of religiousness that we call Indigenous religions these three elements were not yet clearly differentiated. From our present-day perspective, they appear to us to express human religiousness in a more balanced way. That could be the reason why so many people today feel particularly attracted to the spirituality* of Indigenous religions. An additional reason is that our sense of justice revolts against the violation and destruction of Indigenous religions by colonialism. It is an encouraging fact that these ancient traditions with their deep wisdom are coming to new life in many places today and are teaching us a new reverence for nature and for feminine motherly values.

Religion wants to lead religiousness to the joyful outcry, "This is it!" Among the world's great religions, Buddhism* typically zeroes in on silence; the Amen-Traditions* of the West are concerned with the Word; Hinduism* centers on understanding—all forms of yoga* yoking together word and silence. Either one of the three can trigger our "This is it!" We in the West go from one word to another, calling out excitedly, "*This* is it—and *this* and *this* and *this*!" A Buddhist, focused on the one silent Source of all, may put the emphasis on, "This is *it*!" But since meaning is found in both word *and* silence, we may imagine a Hindu emphasizing the understanding that links the two together and exclaiming, "This *is* it!"

14

Faith

Overcoming Fear

Faith is the basic attitude of religiousness—and therefore central also in every religion. Hence, it is an important keyword for orientation. But it is a frequently misunderstood term.

The noun "faith" cannot be as readily transformed into an action-word, as, for example, hope into hoping, or love into loving. The action-word that goes with faith is not "faithing" but believing. And here lies the root for misunderstandings, since believing can stand for two quite different concepts—*opinion* or *trust*. When I say, "I believe that it will rain tomorrow," I express an opinion. When I say, "I believe you," I express trust. The distinction between these two significations of "belief" is a crucial one.

Unfortunately, people usually neglect that distinction when they ask, "Do you believe in God?" They want to get your *opinion*—as if they were asking, "Do you believe in ghosts?" The implication is, "Do ghosts actually exist? What's your opinion as an intelligent person?" But belief in God is not a matter of opinion, in the same sense as belief in ghosts. We have seen that the word "God" stands for "Mystery, under the aspect of our

personal relationship to it." And Mystery is not a matter of opinion. It is an experiential fact. As "that which we cannot grasp, but
understand when it grasps us," we run into Mystery at the core
of everything we encounter in life. If you doubt it, you might as
well doubt that you're alive. Thus, the question "Do you believe
in God?" makes sense only if it means "Do you trust life?"

Do you believe in God? Do you trust the Great Mystery of
Life? These two questions mean exactly the same. But the second way of putting it makes clear that we are asking about trust,
not opinion. It also avoids the G-word, for which there are good
reasons, as we have seen. And it takes us a step further by emphasizing that we have a choice: trust life or fear life. Which of these
two basic attitudes do you choose? One option is faith—trust in
Life and in its Mystery, aka "God." The opposite of faith is not
dis*belief*, but dis*trust*, fearfulness, fear.

Here, we must introduce another important distinction—
between fear and anxiety.* Anxiety is unavoidable in life; fear is
optional. The word "anxiety" has the root meaning "choking,"
and is related to Latin *angustia*, meaning "narrowness." Life inevitably leads us, now and then, into the narrowness of a tight spot.
At those times, we face the choice between trust and fearfulness.
Trust says, "This, too, will pass," identifies the danger, as calmly as
possible, and deals with it as best it can. Fear, in contrast, panics
and spends all its energy resenting the narrowness. When we fear,
we put out bristles of resistance—and thus get stuck in the narrow
spot. If we trust Life, it will carry us through. After all, we came
into this world through the narrow birth canal, and every narrow
spot can become the gateway to a new birth.

In the rear mirror of our life, we can see that our misfortunes,
although they caused us great anxiety at the time, turned into such
"new births." It helps to remember this, especially when, looking
ahead, we see no way through. The choice between fear and trust
ultimately boils down to either insisting that things *ought* to be as

we planned them or entrusting ourselves to the flow of life—not, however, just floating like driftwood, but swimming like fish, wide awake and interacting with the slightest change in the current. Faith collaborates with Life's Mystery, the way a swimmer cooperates with buoyancy, or a dancer with gravity.

In order to experience Mystery, we don't need to believe that it is there and carries us. Likewise, we experience gravity; who needs to believe that it exists? Our balance depends on learning to *trust* gravity and to interact with it; we can be clumsy and awkward or learn to dance on a tightrope. Similarly, orientation in Life depends on how well we learn to play ball, as it were, or dance with Mystery. It demands trust. Faith is ultimately trust in Life. We prove our trust by courageously relying on Mystery at work in every aspect of unfathomable, inexhaustible, unstoppable Life. This is worth repeating. Thus, faith means radical trust in reality—indeed the whole of reality, the inner as well as the outer.

15

Inner/Outer

Two Aspects of One Reality

Outer and inner are two distinct but inseparable dimensions of the one world, as we experience it. The inner we call mind, the outer we call matter. We are reflectively aware of our mind and need that mind in order to be aware of matter. While we can clearly distinguish mind from matter, we must not separate the two. Reducing one aspect of this double realm to the other would fail to respect the experiential fact of the difference between the two; on the other hand, pushing this distinction to the point of separation would contradict the seamless unity of our experience.

We do not know how mind and matter* are related. At any rate, we need to take the objects of our inner experience—the archetypes—as seriously as we take outer objects in the outside world. Here, inner and outer may in fact follow the same pattern. Hermetism knew more than two millennia ago, "As above, so below, and as within, so without." The hypothesis developed by Wolfgang Pauli and C. G. Jung in their correspondence assumes that mind and matter are manifestations of an overarching third, which they call *unus mundus*—One World. This image for the stage on which the whole show is performed, appeals to me personally. But the scholarly exploration of this so-called Hard Problem of Consciousness has been going on for a long time and it continues. In our search for orientation, we need not wait until this or similar problems are solved. It is sufficient to map out firm ground from which we can push forward into unexplored territories. Ancient maps of the world showed unexplored territory as white patches and marked them *terra incognita* (unknown territory), sometimes even *hic sunt dracones* (there are dragons here), since the unknown invites fearful fantasies. Knowing which areas we do know and what we know for sure about them will be a great help in fearlessly exploring the unknown ones.

One of the things we can be sure about is that mind recognizes material reality as clearly distinct from itself and that mind and matter cannot be reduced one to the other. Matter is subject to constant change. Mind has access to the unchanging—say to a triangle with certain unchanging properties—and so we get glimpses of a realm beyond change.

Speculations about mind and matter are of great and lasting interest, but for our orientation, they are relevant only insofar as they concern our awareness of the distinction between our inner and outer experience. That distinction, however, is important indeed, for it reminds us to take both realms seriously and to cultivate our inner life, just like the outer.

Mind, of course, means more than intellect. It includes intuition, volition, emotion. A five-year-old girl got the point. When asked, "What is your mind good for?" she replied, "It's good for keeping secrets." A lie detector may recognize that you want to conceal something; what it is must be guessed at from outer circumstances. No one can look into your mind.

In our materialistic society, we tend to neglect our inner life and get lost in outer concerns. For that reason, it is more important than ever for us, again and again, to return to the now. For only in the now do we experience outer and inner as one.

16

Now

"The Moment in and out of Time"

We usually think of time as a line—the timeline on which the Now is the short section between the past and the future. But how short shall this section be? No matter how short we make it, we can split it again in half. Of these two halves, one is not, because it has passed; it *was*, but *is* no more; the other half is not either, because it only will be in the future, as yet it is not. We can continue forever, dividing our little stretch of present into past and future. The Now, although we clearly experience it, simply cannot be found on our timeline. We can even say, Now is not in time. On the contrary, time is in the Now. How can time be in the Now? Well, the past was once Now; and the future, when it comes, will be Now. "All is always now," says T. S. Eliot in "Burnt Norton." All past and future is somehow present in the now.

Only what is Now actually *is*; what *was* or *will be*, is not. Isn't it amazing: in the midst of transience, we experience something that permanently is—the Now?

The Now is "the intersection of the timeless with time" (T. S. Eliot, "Little Gidding")—the intersection of eternity with time.*

Eternity* is not an endlessly long time, but the opposite pole to time, "the permanent now"—*nunc stans*, as St. Augustine defines eternity. You are living in the double realm: on the outside, you are in the flow of time, but inside of you is "the center of always"—Rilke's name for the Now. "We live—without being aware of it—in the midst of eternity," says Johann Gottfried Herder. And for T. S. Eliot, this time in "The Dry Salvages," the Now, is "the moment in and out of time"—eternity midstream of time.

My I belongs to the realm of space and time. My Self belongs to the realm of eternity. But these two are one inseparable double realm. I-myself am one—not put together of two halves. I must learn to orientate myself in this double realm. This is implied in the phrase "Know yourself!" And the challenge, "Become who you are!" points to the lifetime task of integrating the I and the Self by learning to live in the Now.

The Now is the greatest gift of Life because the given moment contains all other gifts. Kabir prayed that he might be able to hold every moment the way he held his son on the day he was born.

To be in the Now means being fully alive. There is a strange passage in the Hebrew Bible (Deuteronomy 30:19) where God says, "I put before you today, life and death.... Choose life!" Doesn't this sound surprising? Who would not choose life? But the choice is between drifting along in the stream of life and "living deliberately"—which was Henry Thoreau's choice when he went to spend time as a hermit on Walden Pond: "I went to the woods in order to live deliberately." The choice of living deliberately is the key choice each of us will have to make. And this is of such central importance for our orientation that we need to look more closely at the keyword "choice."

17

Choice

What Does Life Want from Me?

All of us have felt the burden of having to make choices. Our experience of inner actions like choosing has to be taken as seriously as that of outer actions before we can investigate our world without prejudice. We need to keep this in mind when science raises the question of whether we can objectively prove freedom* of choice.

Fortunately, as I have said before, we need not wait until such speculative issues are solved. The goal of our inquiry is orientation, and for our orientation, it is sufficient to be aware of well-known ground from which we can push forward into the unknown. Our subjective experience of choosing provides well-known ground indeed. Choice by definition implies freedom. With this in mind, we can explore ways of dealing constructively with our sense of free choice—quite unaffected by the debate to what extent we are free or determined. As Jean-Paul Sartre reminds us, "We are always ready to take refuge in a belief in determinism* when freedom weighs upon us or when we need an excuse."[1]

---

[1] Jean-Paul Sartre, *Being and Nothingness: An Essay in Phenomenological Ontology*, trans. H. E. Barnes (New York: Philosophical Library, 1956), 78–79.

Avoiding excuses, we shall squarely face our subjective sense of freedom and examine concrete situations in which we experience being free—always within limits, but that goes without saying. Let's begin with a special kind of situation in which we are credited by others as acting freely, although we ourselves aren't conscious of making any decision. These are dramatic events in which we don't have time to decide, and yet we spontaneously do exactly what the situation calls for—often with unusual strength and speed. A firefighter jumps into the flames and rescues a person; a mother pulls her child off the rails seconds before a train speeds past. Interviewed afterward, both reject all praise for acting bravely; they did it without any awareness of choice, they insist.

They didn't have "time to think." Time and thinking are two keys for understanding what happened. Thinking needs time. In moments of extreme emergency, the conscious process of thinking would require too much time, and we don't have time. When "we have time," "time has us" in its net. But in a moment when we simply "have no time," "time does not have us" either: suddenly, we are in the Now.

As soon as I am in the Now, I see the appropriate course of action, which organically flows out of the circumstances, and I choose it—have already chosen it, before becoming fully aware of it, in the case of the firefighter and the mother. What happened spontaneously to them in those crucial moments happens more deliberately to anyone of us whenever we are truly in the Now: I and Self act as one—without the effort of choosing, we flow in harmony with the universe.

"How do you mean that?" someone will surely ask. "If the decision flows as soon as I am in the Now, do I have to decide at all?" Of course you have to decide. You are the one who makes the choice. How else could it be *your* choice? And if it is a weighty decision, it may demand a good deal of consideration—consulting others who are affected by your decision, as well as your own deepest desire. And yet the decision is not the result of all those efforts. They are only preparations for the one decisive effort: allowing Life to flow through you.

It is not by chance that both words—con*sidera*tion and desire (from Latin *desiderium*)—make reference to the stars (*sidera* in Latin). Stars played a role in medieval cosmology that might surprise us: seeds were thought to grow into different plants as their response to different stars—a special star for oak trees and a different one for willows, and likewise for all other kinds of plants. This mythic image expresses a lasting truth: there is something like a guiding star also for us humans. That is why people all over the world resonated so strongly with the image of the unreachable star in Joe Darion's lyrics for Don Quixote's lead song in the 1965 musical *The Man of La Mancha*: "To dream the impossible dream . . . To fight the unbeatable foe . . . To bear with unbearable sorrow . . . To run where the brave dare not go . . . To right the unrightable wrong . . . To love pure and chaste from afar . . . To try when your arms are too weary . . . To reach the unreachable star."

Whoever you are, I'm sure you have felt the powerful attraction of that unreachable star as your highest ideal in life. It is stronger than even the highest ambitions that our Ego sets before us. We can easily distinguish between the two: our guiding star makes demands on us that are not what we ourselves would ever come up with. We face these demands by interacting with Life. Our fears want to hang on to the past, our wishful thinking inhabits the future, but only in the Now can we soberly respond to Life and its demands. The Ego is never in the Now, but always entangled in past and future. But by gathering myself into the Now, I come home to myself—my Self.

When we explored the Self, we realized: the Self is one and makes all of us one. As I-myself, I affirm by the way I act that I belong together with all—with all of Life. But this "radical Yes to belonging" is our definition for love. No wonder, then, that the English word "free" comes—like "friend"—from an Indo-European root, *pri*, meaning "to love." And no wonder that St. Augustine sums up right living as, "Love and do what you will." Free choice is not the Ego being able to do what comes into its mind—*willfully*. Genuine freedom *willingly* attunes itself to the innermost guiding principle of Life and of the universe as a whole and flows with it. Eastern wisdom points to this natural flow of things as the *Tao**—"The Watercourse Way,"* as Alan Watts called it. In order to flow in harmony with the Tao, we must recover our original mind, the mind of a child.

When you are still a baby, you are spontaneously both in the flow and in the Now. "There is," as Alan Watts put it, "no you different from what is happening, and therefore it is not happening to you. It is just happening." You are in "the wonderful dancing pattern of liquid ... the patterns of flowing water."[2] As we grow up, we gain reflective consciousness of I and Self, and as this happens, we tend to lose the grace of being in the flow. Yet this loss is not inevitable. Whenever we are in the Now, we are in the flow— and, as adults, consciously and committedly so. As soon as you are in the Now, your choice flows in harmony with the universe— not by some magic,* but quite naturally so. You need only to see things "in the light of your guiding star," to look at the "constellation" of given circumstances, and to spot the opportunity that Life is offering you. Which available course of action seems to promise fulfillment of your deepest, most genuine desire*—the pull of the unreachable star on your heartstrings? That course of action will be the Watercourse Way: everything *"is just happening"*—but now with your adult consent. Your choice—whatever it may be that has to be decided—will not be willful but willingly attuned to the music of life.

---

[2] Alan Watts, "Taoism," available at https://chippit.tripod.com/taoism.html.

One sobering thought, however: we can never be 100 percent sure that our choice is truly in the flow. There always remains a chance that we are deceiving ourselves, a fact that we need humbly to accept—and be glad that there is at least a good chance that we *are* in the flow. There is only one exception: if we feel 100 percent sure that we are right, we can be 100 percent sure that we are wrong. Accepting the fact that our skill in self-deception tends to be well developed, we'll want to do everything we can to counteract it and to develop, instead, full attunement to life. This is the way toward true freedom.

Learning to understand that freeing process better and better and to follow it ever more faithfully is a lifetime task. To many young people, however, making a choice seems to imply losing your freedom. This makes decisive choices particularly difficult. But it need not be so. We explore this next with regard to committing yourself to a vocation.

18

Vocation

"Follow Your Bliss!"

We tend to speak of a vocation when someone's activity obviously implies an especial calling. We speak, for example, of great musicians, outstanding teachers, and dedicated public servants as following their vocation. But everyone has a vocation, namely, what Life is calling us to do. Our English word vocation comes from the Latin *vocare,* which means "to call." With a little extra attention, we can become aware that, moment by moment, Life gives us the opportunity for something and calls for a response from us. Simply put, vocation is on a large scale what the moment-to-moment calls of Life are on a small scale, plus what they add up to in the end.

But how are we going to respond when at a certain moment Life calls us to make plans for the future? How do I find my vocation at that point? Experience shows that we can simplify that process by asking three questions: What is my deepest longing? What am I specially gifted for? What opportunity does Life actually offer me here and now to fulfill my longing and use my gifts? We consider these questions one by one.

At the point of having to choose a career, many young people ask me, "How can I best serve the world?" Their high aspiration makes me happy, and I would like to give an answer that will truly guide and support their choice. I cannot do better, though, than repeat an answer I heard from a spiritual teacher I deeply admire. When a student asked Howard Thurman, "How can I best serve the world?" his answer was essentially: find what really, really gives you joy and do that! The world needs nothing more urgently than people who do with joy what they are doing. Likewise, Joseph Campbell, known for showing how the "Hero's Journey" is the pattern for everyone's life, echoed Thurman's advice by saying succinctly, "Follow your bliss!" Everything depends on not confusing longing with whims and bliss with fun.

If you want to become aware of what this distinction implies for you, you will have to find a quiet place and make time for silence. The image that has often been used for this phase of decision-making is a pond with muddy water. There is nothing you can do to un-muddy it, but if you quietly wait, the mud will settle by itself and gradually you will be able to see what's deep down there. In the same way, inner stillness is necessary if you want to listen to the "small voice within," as Eileen Caddy used to call it. The voice of your deep longing is truly little, soft, and often difficult to hear, because your pet projects make so much noise. Each one of them wants to gain your whole attention. But only by listening to the steady inner voice will you truly be free in your decision. I call that voice "steady" in order to distinguish it from the ever-changing cries of your impulsive wishes. Maybe you could ask yourself, *if all my wishes were fulfilled, what would I still be longing for?*

In order to distinguish your bliss from fun, you will also have to go into silence. What Campbell means by "bliss" implies a lot of things that are anything but fun. What heroic ordeals are you willing to undergo in order to reach the goal of your longing?

Remember that the hero inevitably has to go through a process of dying—cruel dying and even dismemberment, in many forms of the myth—in order to attain the bliss of finding full aliveness and bringing it to others. The little frills you add to the dance give you a kick and are fun. But only your deep attunement to the music and the rhythm, and your attention to the movement of all the other dancers, will give you that fulfillment that deserves to be called bliss.

When you have become aware of your deepest longing, you can ask yourself the second question in planning your future: what are *my* special gifts and talents? It happens sometimes that we get carried away by our admiration for some role model and envisage a future for ourselves for which we are not sufficiently gifted. More often, however, we underestimate our own talents. With work and dedication, even the smallest talents can blossom forth into considerable ability, and no matter how gifted you are, developing your talents requires hard work. With so many people in the world, it may be difficult to believe that your particular combination of longing and gifts is truly unique. But not even your fingerprints find a precise match among those billions of others, how much more your inner life! Your contribution is as necessary for the whole as that of any single instrument for the orchestra. If just one were lacking, the music could not be the same. You want to find your own way, and it will be fully yours, only if you do not imitate somebody else.

Even your shortcomings can trigger unique achievements. If you have to overcome an unhealthy habit, that will give you a moral strength that others who do not have to make that struggle will never develop. Your handicaps also can become a jumping-off point that others lack. Think only of Helen Keller. Were it not for the tragedy of having lost her eyesight and hearing at a very early age, she would never have become the inspiring teacher for millions of people who gratefully admire her.

Keeping both your longing and your gifts consistently in the back of your mind makes you ready to answer the third of our three questions and alert for opportunities you might otherwise have overlooked. Awareness of your genuine longing will be like a compass reading that gives you only the general direction on a hike. The actual terrain to be navigated—obstacles and opportunities—is what Life is offering you at any given moment.

In many places of the world, the social arrangements give some young people so many options that they feel overwhelmed. The vast majority, however, have only a very narrow margin of opportunities. Millions of youngsters have no choice at all; they must concentrate on day-by-day survival. We must make every effort to change an unjust social order that offends in this way against human dignity.

What matters most, however, is available to everyone. It is not *what* you do, but *how* you do it; not your position in the circle of dancers, but the way you dance—with attention and respect for all others, but especially for the ones next to you. It is too easy for us to feel compassion for those far away while overlooking those with whom we have to deal daily. Through those with whom we hold hands do we reach all other dancers in the circle.

Now suppose you have become aware of your genuine longing, have correctly evaluated your talents, and are following, step by step, the path that life is opening up before you. This is what it means to find your bliss—to follow your vocation. However, you won't get very far on that path before Life is asking for a commitment of one kind or another.

19

Commitment

What Can Make It Last?

The very idea of commitment presents a frightening challenge for many people today. This is a problem we have to face head-on. What is it that makes lasting—maybe even lifelong—commitment to a task or a relationship so difficult for us? To start with, we may list three of the main reasons: the increasing length of human life expectancy, the change that every aspect of life is undergoing, and—closely connected with the speed of that change—a kind of all-pervading anxiousness.* How can we deal with these three facts that make commitment so challenging today?

Of course, a longer life is something desirable. It gives us the opportunity to accomplish in one lifetime what would have taken two or three lifetimes not many generations ago. But how can you maintain your commitment over so long a time when circumstances keep changing as dramatically as they often do? We need to distinguish our commitment from the particular form it takes. That form can change over time while the commitment itself does not change. Our grandparents did not make that distinction: a long-term commitment was simply understood to mean commitment to one and the same form. To us, the flexibility and readiness for change in our society give more options. Today it is possible to live out one lifelong commitment in a variety of successive forms. We commit ourselves to realizing our goal in life, not to one particular form of doing so. For example, we can pursue two or three careers successively, using a variety of our talents, while staying faithful to our deepest longing. One may attend to the same goal of creating a fairer society while being, in succession, an activist in a nongovernmental organization, a politician, and a teacher to younger generations. One may unswervingly remain devoted to environmental justice as a gardener, then as a vegan cook, and finally as a senior citizen faithfully signing petitions on the internet and forwarding them to a network of friends.

The third obstacle to commitment, we called it *anxiousness*, expresses itself in an all-pervasive restlessness. Increasingly, the media use rapid-fire news reporting in order to satisfy our insatiable thirst for ever-new stimuli. Fewer and fewer people still read long text passages that try to do justice to a subject; input has to be cut down to sound bites because of our short attention span—which is getting ever shorter. When we send a message, we want an instantaneous answer. Any process that takes time makes us anxious. We have lost the joy that comes only when we have to wait for something—the joy of deferred gratification, as it is called. As a result, we have a sick relationship to time—an anxious sense that time is running out and our life with it. "I'm running out, I'm running out, like sand that's running through my fingers," a young man complains in one of Rilke's poems. However, time is merely the rhythmic beat of Life, and we can learn to dance to it. "I said to my soul, be still, and wait," writes T. S. Eliot in "East Coker." He is well aware that stillness can cause anxiousness; we need noise to distract us from our threatening inner darkness. No fear, says Eliot: you can trust the darkness of your inner stillness. And he closes that section of the poem with the assurance that "the darkness shall be the light, and the stillness the dancing."

Thus, if we want to regain a healthy relationship to time, the first step is to become aware that we are out of step with the natural rhythm of Life. Next, we need to build moments of stillness into our day, maybe certain times in which we shut off all our screens. By turning our attention inward instead of outward, we cleanse our vision and attune our hearts to the guidance of that "small voice of silence." It will guide us to something we rightly desire: the joy of leisure.* Leisure is not the privilege of those who can afford to *take* time for it, but the achievement of those who *give* time to whatever they are doing—as much time as it deserves, no more and no less. If we strive for leisure, we will find our rhythm for communicating, for being alone, for working, eating, sleeping, and everything we do. We will find our rhythm as dancers.

One implication of our dance imagery is that each individual dancer is part of the whole. Have you caught yourself saying, "This is *my* life. I can do with it whatever I want"? This puts an enormous burden on you, for if you can *do* what you want, you have to figure out *what it is* that you want. No wonder this fills you with anxiousness. In reality, things are much simpler. Your life and the life of all others are inseparably intertwined, and you can rely on Life to tell you what to do with your share in it. Our contemporary sense of personal freedom is a great historic achievement for which many have suffered and died. We inherited this gift, but we have pushed it too far—so far that we are lost in alienation. The challenge before us is to treasure and preserve the *in*dependence given to us and learn to integrate it in an all-embracing *inter*dependence. Universal inter-independence is the pattern of Life, and we may entrust ourselves to Life and to Mystery at its core.

There are occasions when that trust is clearly acknowledged and solemnly expressed: moments of mutual commitment with another person or a whole community. In those cases, the commitment can, in fact, be for life. This can happen only when those who freely commit themselves to each other see their mutual belonging with such inner clarity that they can promise each other to preserve that relationship, come what may. Such sacred moments—for that is what they are—have since ancient times been marked by solemn rituals. One might think that those who consecrate themselves to one another by so weighty and far-reaching a commitment are promising each other to stick it out together, come what may. But actually, those are moments in which they entrust themselves to Life's promise to see them through, come what may. What comes will surely not be an easy ride; a minimum of realism tells us that. Commitment of this kind demands sacrifice—a repeated dying into ever-greater richness of aliveness. If Life leads you to this kind of commitment—a vow for life—this will be a great gift, though probably a rare one.

Thinking of a lifelong commitment may frighten most anyone, but even the longest life is merely a sequence of moments. So even a longtime commitment is lived out as a moment-by-moment one. Living out any commitment in daily life follows a three-step pattern we discuss in the next section. It will be a "Stop! Look! Go!"—practiced and renewed over and over again.

20

Stop! Look! Go!

Three Steps of the Great Dance

These three words form a rule that helps children cross the street safely. It is also the simplest formula for navigating daily life safely by practicing grateful living.* Let's look at these three powerful words, one by one.

Stop!

Everything else depends on this first step. It can take us out of an automatism of which we are not even aware and make us, as if for the first time, come alive. Learning to stop and be still is absolutely necessary before we can listen and respond fully and gratefully to Life—moment by moment. Stop!—as we are here using this word—means simply to hold still. All of us are so used to clatter and commotion, around us and within us, that we might feel a bit uncomfortable with stillness. But we can practice being still—a little longer every day. Through practice, we will progressively feel at home in stillness. If right action is our goal, stillness must be our starting point.

Stop! is not an idle stopping. It is "mostly standing and learning," as the first step toward the only work that really matters.

Standing in stillness enables "the ears of your heart," as St. Benedict calls them, to listen deeply to Life and again and again be astonished. Only in silence can you listen; only once you Stop! can you truly Look!

Look!

Anchored in your inner stillness, you can—now, as a second step—pay full attention to everything that the moment contains. Stopping in silence gives your way of looking at things time "to ripen," as Rilke puts it, and now, "everything you look at, comes toward you like a bride."

Normally we are not even aware of how violently we are taking hold of things, simply by the way we look at them. But we can learn to let our glances reverently embrace everything we see, as a bridegroom embraces a bride—and flows into her embrace. All our senses can learn this give-and-take approach to the world around us. Then the opportunity we are looking for—in the context of Look!—will not primarily be an opportunity to *use* what Life is offering us at this moment, but to *enjoy* it. Then everything we do, even our work,* can turn into joyful play.*

Frances Cornford celebrates the bridal, loving way of Look! in the "attentive courtesy" with which a guitarist tunes his instrument:

> *With what attentive courtesy he bent*
> *Over his instrument;*
> *Not as a lordly conqueror who could*
> *Command both the wire and wood,*
> *But as a man with a loved woman might*

Inquiring with delight
What slight essential things she had to say
Before they started, he and she, to play.[1]

Go!

Go! will be "play" if the Look! that leads up to it is at the same time the listening of a lover—an "inquiring" into what Life "has to say" to us at this moment. The Go! that springs from this attitude will be "playful." It will be intense action but it will appear effortless. Why? Because it is a response that takes even "slight" hints of Life seriously, knowing that they are "essential things"—essential for our action to be attuned to Life, and that's what ultimately matters. When we act in tune with Life, Life's music flows through us, giving our Go! both beauty and power. Whether you are pruning tomato plants, writing your résumé, ironing a shirt, or participating in a conference call, "good work" will be "like a sacred dance."

Chuang Tzu uses this dance image in Thomas Merton's poem "Cutting Up an Ox." The work of a meat-cutter was an utterly despised activity in Chuang Tzu's society, and yet, after watching it, Prince Wen Hui calls out excitedly, "This is it!" It was one of those aha moments for him. "This is it! My cook has shown me how I ought to live my own life!" Twenty-three centuries later, we can say the same, because the way Prince Wen Hui's cook is cutting up an ox follows the way of the Tao, the Watercourse Way, and that remains, throughout the ages, the way of the perfect Go! "guided by natural line."

"True, there are sometimes tough joints"—tough spots in the Go! But the cook teaches us how to deal with them. "I

---

[1] Frances Darwin Cornford, "The Guitarist Tunes Up," available at https://allpoetry.com/The-Guitarist-Tunes-Up.

feel them coming, I slow down" (so he goes back to Stop!); "I watch closely" (he goes back to Look!), and then, I "hold back, barely move the blade"—his Go! is now flowing with the energy of Life itself. "The spirit, free to work without plan, follows its own instinct, guided by natural line." Let us savor the whole poem.

"Cutting Up an Ox"

Prince Wen Hui's cook
Was cutting up an ox.
Out went a hand,
Down went a shoulder,
He planted a foot,
He pressed with a knee,
The ox fell apart
With a whisper,
The bright cleaver murmured
Like a gentle wind.
Rhythm! Timing!
Like a sacred dance,
Like "The Mulberry Grove,"
Like ancient harmonies!

"Good work!" the Prince exclaimed,
"Your method is faultless!"
"Method?" said the cook
Laying aside his cleaver,
"What I follow is Tao
Beyond all methods!

"When I first began
To cut up an oxen
I would see before me
The whole ox
All in one mass.

"After three years
I no longer saw this mass.
I saw the distinctions.

"But now, I see nothing
With the eye. My whole being
Apprehends.
My senses are idle. The spirit
Free to work without plan
Follows its own instinct
Guided by natural line,
By the secret opening, the hidden space,
My cleaver finds its own way.
I cut through no joint, chop no bone.

"A good cook needs a new chopper
Once a year—he cuts.
A poor cook needs a new one
Every month—he hacks!

"I have used this same cleaver
Nineteen years.
It has cut up
A thousand oxen.
Its edge is as keen
As if newly sharpened.

"There are spaces in the joints;
The blade is thin and keen:
When this thinness
Finds that space
There is all the room you need!
It goes like a breeze!
Hence, I have this cleaver nineteen years
As if newly sharpened!

"True, there are sometimes
Tough joints. I feel them coming,
I slow down, I watch closely,
Hold back, barely move the blade,
And whump! the part falls away
Landing like a clod of earth.

"Then I withdraw the blade,
I stand still
And let the joy of the work
Sink in.
I clean the blade
And put it away."

Prince Wan Hui said,
"This is it! My cook has shown me
How I ought to live
My own life!"[2]

---

[2] Thomas Merton, *The Collected Poems of Thomas Merton* (New York: New Directions, 1977), 872–74.

On a long Greyhound bus ride, I once had the privilege of sitting next to a meat-cutter who told me of his work. He certainly had never heard of Taoism, let alone the Chuang Tzu poem, but I could hardly believe how closely the proud description he gave of his skill resembled that of his Taoist colleague of so long ago. This no longer surprises me. I've come to realize that our Stop! Look! Go! is not a method someone invented, but the timeless way—"way" is what *Tao* literally means—of living in harmony with the universe. As the poet said,

> *"Method?" said the cook*
> *Laying aside his cleaver,*
> *"What I follow is Tao*
> *Beyond all methods!"*

The Watercourse Way is beyond all methods, yet reaching this goal requires conscientious training through some spiritual practice. Every spiritual practice I have come to know aims at the same goal: living in the Now. This holds true also of Stop! Look! Go! and makes it—simple though it is—a full-fledged spiritual practice. Simple does not mean easy; you'll have to practice Stop! Look! Go! again and again. Still, its simplicity gives it a great advantage over other spiritual practices: it does not require any special setting; you can practice it anyplace, anytime—at your workplace as well as in your prayer corner, on the subway as well as on a hike in the mountains. And whenever you practice that simple three-step process, it will bring you into the Now. You can *look* gratefully at past and future, but whenever you *are* grateful, it is now.

And why is that so important? Because the Ego cannot survive in the Now. The Ego is always entangled with the past—feeling itself a victim, regretting past guilt, or dwelling on the "good old times"—or ensnared by the future—impatiently waiting for it or frightened by it. Finding the Now means gathering our scattered Ego into "the center of always" within us. Thus, through Stop! Look! Go!, we return home—from Ego to I-myself, from illusion to reality.

Thus, orientation becomes possible—orientation in relation to reality and to Mystery as the ultimate Reality. Whenever you Stop!, ever so briefly, you touch Mystery under its aspect of Silence. Whenever you Look! and listen in that posture of inner stillness, the ears of your heart are attuned to the Word that comes out of Silence and speaks to you in and through everything there is. And whenever you respond by your action to that Word—be it a person, an animal, a plant, a thing, a pleasure, a challenge, or whatever opportunity—you will find meaning; and thus this process of orientation will bring you back into stillness, for meaning is that within which the heart finds rest.

Through Stop!, we practice the first and most basic step toward finding meaning: trust in Life. That trust takes courage. All our frantic activities are merely anxious attempts to stay in control. Whether or not we are aware of it, they are fake alibis, excuses from facing Life's real challenges. When we consciously stop, we recognize that what is truly meaningful are not our own hectic plans but quiet trust in Life. Faith is the traditional name of that radical trust.

Through Look!, we practice the attitude traditionally called hope.* Hope differs from our hopes (in the plural), for these are always expectantly directed toward something we can imagine. *Hope is radical openness for surprise*—for the unimaginable. If that is the attitude with which we look, listen, and open all our senses, we enter into a meaningful relationship with whatever Life offers us at a given moment.

Through Go!, we enter into interaction with everything else, and that means saying—or rather acting—*a radical Yes to belonging*. And this is our definition for *Love*.

Just as the attitude of Faith differs from beliefs, and hope differs from hopes, Love differs from our likes. Faith, hope, and Love are ultimately directed toward Mystery. Stop! Look! Go! renews, again and again, our relationship toward Mystery as our most basic orientation in Life.

In a poem of no more than ten lines, Rilke leads us through those three steps—from the stillness of Stop! through the vision of Look! to the joyful doing of Go! Praying for outer and inner stillness, the poet imagines that this would give his watching such powerful concentration that his inner eye could reach the edge of Mystery. He even speaks of *holding* that vision—though only for the duration of a smile. Who would not smile at the idea that one could hold on to Mystery? But now his looking turns into the most joyful doing, as he lavishes with abandon what he has seen on all the world "as a thanksgiving."

> *If only things would be completely still for once.*
> *If all that is haphazard and irrelevant*
> *fell silent, like the neighbors' laughter.*
> *And if the background noise my senses make*
> *Did not distract me so from watching—*
>
> *I might, then, with a thousand-fold*
> *thought's outreach touch your outer limit*
> *and hold you, but no longer than a smile,*
> *then, squander you on everything that's living*
> *as a thanksgiving.*

Any child can follow our simple three steps of Stop! Look! Go!, yet this is a powerful tool for finding orientation and joy in Life through grateful living.

21

Grateful Living

A Path toward Life in Fullness

Gratitude and thanksgiving spring up spontaneously in our heart when we are overjoyed by a gift we received. In this section, however, we are concerned not with a momentary emotion, but with a permanent attitude: grateful living.

Grateful living provides an ingeniously simple gateway to living fully and joyfully. Better than anything else, it can help us find our orientation—and find it again every time we lose it.

All people on Earth know what it means to be grateful. All cultures treasure gratitude. All religions emphasize its fundamental importance. All wisdom traditions praise it highly. Since its beginnings, philosophy in the East and West has been seeking guidelines for the good life. Cicero held that "gratitude is not only the greatest of virtues, but the parent of all others." This makes gratitude a powerful force. And since grateful living is accessible to all human beings, it offers to the whole human family a shared path toward Life in fullness.

But what exactly do we mean by "grateful living"? It starts with gratitude. In daily experience, we find that gratitude arises spontaneously within us, as we said, whenever we receive something desirable as a pure gift. These two elements must come together in our awareness: we feel that we didn't earn or deserve this, and at the same time, it is of great value to us. The higher we value the gift and the less we deserve it, the stronger the trigger that releases gratitude. Suppose, as it sometimes happens, you arrive for a dreaded operation and a final checkup reveals that the cancer has disappeared without a trace. You are overwhelmed by relief and joy, humbled—but in no way humiliated—by a sense of being undeservedly privileged, spontaneously eager to show yourself worthy of what you received, and to share with others this abundance of intense aliveness. We need not wait for such an extraordinary demonstration.

When we wake up from taking everything for granted, we realize that the most precious gift of all—Life—gives itself to us lavishly and undeservedly at every moment, no less so than to the patient in our story at the moment the surgery was called off. Let this awareness sink in. It may take awhile. When it does, it will fill your heart with overflowing gratitude. You will suddenly feel truly alive, better, more yourself—joyfully glowing inside and radiating that joy. You will want to share the gift of Life fully and gratefully. You will have found an inner orientation toward full aliveness. Even though we cannot avoid bouts of forgetfulness now and then, from now on, your goal will be grateful living, regardless of what Life might have in store for you.

But maybe we are looking through rose-colored glasses. Can we really be grateful for *everything* that Life gives us? The answer is clearly, no! There are many things for which no one can be grateful, yet we can be grateful at every moment if we know what the real gift is. The gift within every gift is opportunity. Both kinds of gift—the gifts for which we can be grateful and those for which we can't—contain that real gift: opportunity. It is for this opportunity that we are grateful. Most of the time, it is the opportunity to enjoy. We notice this only when we start practicing. Gradually we become aware what great gifts we used to simply take for granted. Our senses wake up and recognize the countless opportunities to see, hear, smell, taste, and touch as sources of joy to which we had hardly been paying attention.

Even at times when something happens to us for which we cannot be grateful—say, lies, harassment, or infidelity in private life; or violence, oppression, or exploitation in public life— everything is offering us the gift of opportunity. It may be the opportunity to grow inwardly, to learn patience and compassion, to forgive, or to stand up and protest—peacefully but with determination. And for these opportunities we can indeed be grateful, difficult though it may be at first to recognize them for what they are. Even when we do recognize an opportunity, we can still find it difficult to *feel* grateful for it. *Feeling* is not what provides gratitude but action—the action of using the opportunity given to us creatively.

But—another objection—even if we manage to be grateful for the opportunity, can we *enjoy* that gift within a gift for which no one can be grateful? Yes, we can. We may not be happy—most likely, in fact, we will not be happy—but joy* is more than happiness.* Joy is the happiness that does not depend on what happens. That is the happiness our heart is longing for: *lasting* happiness. Only grateful living can give you that joy because it gives meaning to Life. You are holding the key to it in your own hands. Health turns into sickness, wealth into poverty, fortune into misfortune. But amid all these ups and downs, grateful living fills our heart with a steady, calm joy. You can't be happy when you are lying in bed with a serious illness. But you can face that situation creatively: you can focus on new opportunities that this situation is giving you, and so find joy.

Every opportunity for which we are grateful triggers joy within us, even in the midst of misfortune. Due to an extraordinarily

serious cancer, my young friend Claudia came into contact with
an organization—Fundación Salud—that helps such seriously ill
people switch to a healthy diet; practice healthy breathing; learn
to meditate, play, and dance; and heal failed relationships. This
helped her put life in order. Skeptical at first, Claudia admitted
after a few months, "I am truly grateful. Every day of my illness
is giving me new opportunities for joy. I am learning to change
bad habits, and to discover an altogether new aliveness." Although
most people would have given up at the time, Claudia is now fully
recovered: even a physical cure took place in her case. What takes
place in every case, however, matters most: the spiritual healing
that grateful living brings.

We tend to think that happiness makes us grateful. But look
carefully. It is the other way around: grateful living makes us
happy. Most likely you know people who have everything we
associate with happiness, yet they are anything but happy. And
you may know others who, in the midst of misfortune, radiate
joy. Why? Because the ones are grateful in spite of all, while the
others feel entitled to good fortune and always remain dissatisfied.
This sense of entitlement,* so widespread in our society—even
the urban poor are affected by it—is diametrically opposed to
grateful living.

It often happens that tourists from economically privileged
countries are amazed by the radiant joy of people in poorer
countries, people who lack even the essentials. Can you guess the
reason for that joy? Pay attention once more to the way in which
the joy of gratitude arises in your own heart. Don't you feel that
your appreciation for the gift—whatever it may be—is surging
within you, quietly filling your heart to the point of overflowing?
That's the decisive point—like the point at which water silently
rising in the basin of a fountain suddenly brims over, pattering,
splattering, and glittering in the sunlight. In an affluent society
that glorious moment never comes. Just when appreciation wants

to spill over into joy, advertising stops the joyous bubbling by persuading us that we ought to have a bigger and better and newer model. Competitive comparison ruins everything. Just when the bowl wants to overflow, we make it bigger—and bigger again. *Affluence** literally means the result of flowing toward—without overflowing. Those poor people who are not yet affected by consumerism and the sense of entitlement have very small bowls; one drop is enough to make them overflow with delight.

This joy can be ours, too. Grateful living can heal us from the sense of entitlement by helping us to master the art of frugal* living, and so free us from consumerism. Frugal living means intentional living—awake, alert, and oriented toward goals of one's own choice.

Unfortunately, we must admit that our society is neither frugal nor grateful. Consumerism, competitive comparison, and an entitlement mentality are spreading everywhere. We are taking for granted what our grandparents would have considered unbelievable abundance. Modern economies have paradoxically reversed their objective, putting greater effort into *creating* new needs rather than into *fulfilling* the real ones. Incited by the deceptive machinery of advertising, we want more and more, take it for granted, and so enjoy less and less. Only grateful living triggers lasting joy by giving meaning to our life. But we are asleep. If we were awake, we would recognize everything there is as a gift of Life. Only gratitude toward the Mystery of Life can give a firm center of meaning to our culture. We have lost awareness of that center. The joy of a meaningful life depends on regaining it.

W. B. Yeats shows us how we lost awareness of Mystery at the center. He uses the image of a falcon gyrating in wider and wider circles until it is out of earshot to the falconer's whistle. When our relationship to Mystery is lost, "Mere anarchy is loosed upon the world." Then "the blood-dimmed tide" of violence is drowning "the ceremony of innocence" that is—in Rilke's words, quoted earlier—"existence still enchanted, still beginning in a hundred places." Here is the first stanza of Yeats's famous poem "The Second Coming":

> *Turning and turning in the widening gyre*
> *The falcon cannot hear the falconer;*
> *Things fall apart; the centre cannot hold;*
> *Mere anarchy is loosed upon the world,*
> *The blood-dimmed tide is loosed, and everywhere*
> *The ceremony of innocence is drowned;*
> *The best lack all conviction, while the worst*
> *Are full of passionate intensity.*

In this powerful statement, the last two lines frighten me most, for I ask myself, *Are we among "the best" who "lack all conviction"?* If so, let us listen to Christopher Fry's verse as a wake-up call, a rallying cry:

> *Thank God our time is now when wrong*
> *Comes up to face us everywhere,*
> *Never to leave us till we take*
> *The longest stride of soul we ever took*
>
> *Affairs are now soul size*
> *The enterprise*
> *Is exploration into God.*[1]

The "soul size" task that faces us today is reorienting ourselves amid a disoriented society, through finding again our relationship to Mystery (Fry calls it "God"). We have seen how our Stop! Look! Go!—if we live it at its deepest level—helps us

---

[1] Christopher Fry, from *A Sleep of Prisoners* (New York: Oxford University Press, 1954).

find this reorientation moment by moment; this works even when we aren't explicitly thinking of it. But this takes firm conviction and great inner strength; it demands spiritual backbone.* Only the deepest of our relationships—our relationship with Mystery— can strengthen our backbone sufficiently to stand up against the pressure of society. Once our personal practice of grateful living has given us this strength, our own inner transformation will be a first step toward transforming society as a whole. And this is urgently necessary, for "wrong comes up to face us everywhere." We are living at a moment in history when the ego-created "System" confronts our society with the gravest choice: self-trans-formation or self-annihilation.

Grateful living has power steering. It can bring about the U-turn we need. The power pyramid is built by fear. Grateful living is powered by trust. The fearful Ego needs to resort to vio-lence. The healthy I can afford nonviolence* because it trusts in life. Trust turns rivalry into cooperation, greed into sharing, and the power pyramid* itself into a network of networks. This is the revolution we need—a revolution that revolutionizes even the very notion of revolution. No longer will revolution mean that those who were at the bottom of the pyramid now get to the top and behave just like those who were on top before them. There will be no more top. Power will no longer be able to hijack authority;* instead, authority based on wisdom will bestow power. Those with authoritative insight will be given positions of power as long as their service is needed and for no longer.

These changes may sound utopian, but they are necessary for our survival—and much more than mere survival. Grateful living deepens mindfulness through an important component, namely mutuality. Mindfulness in splendid isolation can be quite egocen-tric. As we saw all along, it is through relationships that we find meaning and orientation in life. Mutuality gives grateful living its revolutionary power. Imagine a society in which mutual trust has the leverage that our present social order accords to fear. Imagine a society in which mutual caring has the leverage that our present social order accords to egotism. If we reach a critical mass of grateful people, a surprising reorientation can take place.

Grateful living can build the kind of world for which every human heart is longing. Its life force is the force of Life itself— the power of Mystery. It pulsates through the universe, ready to transform our own lives and the life of society as soon as we open our hearts to it.

This, then, would be—using imagery with which we are familiar—Yeats's falcon learning to listen so intensely that it can hear the falconer and yet draw ever-wider circles. This would transform, in turn, the widening gyres of its flight into the great circle dance around Mystery that *sits in the center and knows*. For each of us and for society as a whole, this would mean—in the full sense of the word—finding orientation.

Annotations to Some of
Our Keywords

AFFLUENCE

Wherever we look we find societies and individuals trying to become affluent. If this means having enough and maybe even a little more than enough, it is a good thing as long as that little more is being passed on to others who are in need of it. Simply having things does not really make you happy but rather anxious of losing them. The real joy of having enough comes with sharing. In most affluent societies, however, fear* leads to never-ending accumulation and so the joy of sharing never comes.

Whatever we do not need—and make generous allowance for the meaning of "need"—life wants us to give away, because life wants our joy. Affluence means literally *flowing toward,* but it is not enough that things flow toward us for the sake of our happiness; they must overflow. The current notion of affluence is based on a sense of scarcity—there is not enough for all. For our true happiness it needs to be replaced by a concept that springs from a sense of life's abundance. Abundance literally means *overflowing.* The task before us is a shift of consciousness: from the fearful attitude behind affluence to the trust in Life that leads to joyful abundance.

AFTERLIFE

In ordinary consciousness, we are aware that the mind-body entity we call "I" must die; yet in altered states of consciousness—in peak experiences, near-death experiences, or meditation, or under the influence of drugs—we can become aware of living also in a different dimension, one that is beyond death, because it is beyond our mind-body existence in space-time. We call that dimension our Self. Just as we can think of our mind as the "inside view" of our bodily existence, so we can imagine our Self as the "inside view" of our mind-body existence. I observe myself—mind and body—from the viewpoint of my Self and recognize: I must die. But the Self the Observer is not bound by space-time and is, thus, beyond death. Thus, "I-myself" am living in both a mortal and an immortal dimension.

When we keep all this in mind and think about our death, we can come to understand how the notion originated of an immortal soul as some part of ourselves that will survive death. It was an attempt to acknowledge that we must die and yet do justice to our awareness that paradoxically we are both mortal and immortal. Yet it is not part of ourselves, but our whole *mortal* body-mind that has an *immortal* dimension—here and now. And we can cultivate an awareness of our immortal Self in our normal state of consciousness. In fact, the more our I stays aware of our Self, the more we find peace of mind. We can experience that peace of heart in this life, and it will make us less preoccupied with an afterlife.

The term "afterlife" is problematic anyway. Death comes when "our time is up": time, as we know it, comes to an end. So, what should there be "after" time? It might be better to speak of a "beyond-life." We can actually experience *before* death, as we have seen, a dimension of our being that goes beyond the boundaries of our mind-body existence and so beyond death; we need only cultivate a mindfulness that stays alert to the Self. For a consciousness of that kind, dying may be more like the "death" of a caterpillar in its cocoon and its emergence as a butterfly. We don't know. We grope for images, and the comparison with metamorphosis proves helpful to many people.

The concern for life beyond death is often triggered by the question, will we be reunited with our loved ones who have died? Deep love is certainly an attitude not only of our mind-body I but of our innermost Self. And since the Self is imperishable, so is love. This, however, is cold comfort, because it is cold logic, and the question about reunion with our loved ones is not merely intellectual but highly charged with emotions. Wishful thinking won't get us any closer to certainty, but there is something that will. Here and now, we can strengthen our bonds of love, cultivate and celebrate our awareness that those bonds unite us at the center of our innermost Self. If we do this diligently in daily life, we will hardly have time for idle speculations about an afterlife. The hearts of lovers who practice this love will "rest in peace," here and now, without worrying about hereafter. (See also Soul, Death)

AMEN TRADITIONS

In this book, we use the term "Amen Traditions" to refer to Judaism, Christianity, and Islam together. It is no accident that *Amen* is an important word in these three traditions. The central concern of all three of them is our relationship to God,* more precisely, trust in God. And trust is exactly the meaning of the Hebrew word *amen*. It is the human "yes!" to the divine *Amunah*, the Hebrew word for God's absolute reliability. Psalm 130:5b expresses most succinctly what Amen means: "I trust in His word." Whatever the present moment contains can be understood as the word by which God speaks to us. If we trust that word and express our trust through our response, each moment can become a joyful Amen.

ANXIETY

Anxiety, anxiousness,* and fear* are three different concepts that need to be carefully distinguished. Anxiety is our reaction to a perceived threat. There is nothing we can do to avoid it.

It arises spontaneously and often causes bodily changes like an outpouring of adrenaline in our system. We may feel that we can hardly breathe: our chest is contracting, and our throat is closing. This sense of narrowness is behind the Latin word *angustia,* from which the English "anxiety" derives. When we get anxious we have two choices: we can calmly face the frightening situation, reasonably respond to the threat (in a human version of the instinctive "fight-or-flight" pattern), and so pass through the narrow spot; or else we can fearfully react with an arrogant "Why me?" attitude, put up our inner bristles of resistance, and get stuck in the narrow place. Life leads us again and again into tight spots. We cannot avoid them, but we can learn to pass through them courageously. Anxiety is unavoidable, but fear is optional. The difference between courage and fear hinges ultimately on trust in life, or the lack of it. Fear is lack of trust.

The original experience of anxiety is our birth, subconsciously remembered. The original narrowness through which we have to go is the birth canal. The trust we instinctively showed during our birth process, Life asks from us again and again, but now consciously, by following the Watercourse Way.* As often as we face and brave anxiety with trust, anxiety leads to a new birth. Throughout the ages, humans have somehow felt that even the anxiety of death pangs may be a birth process into a new life that we cannot yet imagine—as little as a caterpillar can imagine life as a butterfly.

ANXIOUSNESS

Anxiousness is a form of low-intensity anxiety, but it is so distinct that we need a special term for it. Anxiousness is typically vague, unfocused, long-lasting, and debilitating, shading over into depression. Unfortunately, anxiousness has become the normal state for many people today, even children, for two main reasons. Both spring from our preoccupation with the future and our constant anticipation of it. On the one hand, we feel threatened by the future. Being always unpredictable, the future inevitably contains an element of threat. This threat, often quite nebulous, causes anxiousness to be a general sense of insecurity in the face of the future.

On the other hand, we are impatient for the future to arrive. The ever-growing speed and pressure of our daily lives make us more and more preoccupied with things to come. This exposes the other face of anxiousness: the unceasing dissatisfaction caused by a vague sense that something is missing in our life today, combined with the unrealistic expectation that this will be solved by some future event.

Both these aspects can be overcome by learning to live in the now,* tasting the present moment to the full.

AUTHORITY

Most people think of authority in the first place as power to command. But rightly understood, however, authority is more deeply seated; it is what gives you the *right* to command. A person with authority is one who taps into the source of clear insight and appropriate action—in other words, someone who possesses wisdom.

True authority leads through wisdom.* It proves itself by clear insight into the meaning of a given situation and clear vision of the goal to be achieved. A wise leader acts not as an impetuous führer, but as a patient midwife, bringing to birth in people's hearts attitudes that enable them to live together peacefully and joyfully.

AWE

Awe is the strange sense of bewilderment that rises in the human heart when we are confronted with the holy.* (More about this aspect under Religiousness.*) What characterizes spiritually mature people is awe not just as an occasional experience but as a permanent attitude because they are aware of the presence of Mystery in everything they encounter. In the encounter with other humans, awe springs up as awareness of their human dignity.* We need to cultivate this sense of awe today because it has been lost, with detrimental consequences for society.

Through their readiness to be surprised by things we overlook because we take them for granted, children can teach us. Their capacity to be surprised is an important ingredient of awe.

BACKBONE

In anatomy we call it the spinal cord, but colloquially we speak of the backbone. A healthy backbone gives you strength for physical labor; thus, "putting one's backbone into something" has come to mean getting some bodily work done. When a car is stuck in the mud, "put your backbone into it and push!" But we use the expression also in a transferred sense, for people who stand by their principles, even against resistance and pressure: "The party put its backbone into it and pushed the bill through." A sturdy backbone helps you stand firmly upright. Therefore, we say of a woman who acts with strength, integrity, and self-confidence, "She shows her backbone." In our quest for spiritual orientation, we do well to remember the saying, "Success depends on your backbone, not your wishbone."

For billions of years, before the inner skeleton with its spinal cord evolved, nature knew only the so-called external skeleton. We can still observe it today, as the shell of lobsters and crabs or as the chitinous armor of beetles. An outer skeleton gives protection and support to the body, but it hinders growth: the larvae of beetles must shed their shells more than a dozen times as they grow to their full size. An outer skeleton also hampers movement. You have surely seen a beetle lying on its back, struggling to get on its feet. Through an internal skeleton the body gains a new ease of growth and mobility.

Today we are experiencing an evolutionary step in human consciousness, comparable to physical evolution's step from an outer to an inner skeleton. Not so long ago in history, an individual's choices in life were largely determined by society's expectations, by generally accepted rigid rules intended to shore up "proper" behavior "from the outside," as it were. But today, external codes of conduct are rapidly losing their binding power; instead, inner integrity will have to keep us upright. The rigid parts of a corset are called its "bones." A new consciousness is challenging us to replace the bones of a social corset with our personal backbone.

World history offers us shining examples of prophetic figures who showed their backbone. Hildegard of Bingen stood her ground as a woman against a world of imperious men, and Catherine of Siena put even the pope—gently, but firmly—in his place. Like them, we need a strong, flexible backbone to join in the Great Dance of Life.

BELIEF

Belief is a term generally used with two quite different meanings that need to be carefully distinguished. In everyday language, belief means uncertainty with regard to an unknown outcome: "I believe the Rangers will win the game." In a spiritual context, to believe means primarily to trust, as in the formulations of a religious creed: "I believe in God," and so on. The Apostles' Creed, for example, is not a series of facts to be believed but a series of images for different aspects of the believers' faith/trust.

When you "believe in a friend," in the sense of trusting him or her, you also have certain beliefs and opinions about them. Correspondingly, religious trust/belief leads to certain beliefs, but they are as secondary with regard to your faith/trust as the opinion you have about your friends.

BIG PICTURE*

BLESSING*

BODY

The body is defined as the organized physical configuration of an animal or plant. Speaking of humans, it usually means the living body, as distinguished from a corpse.

We can think of our body as having a mind that asks questions that open out into Mystery. From this perspective, we might consider the body to be an outer layer, with mind or psyche as an inner one, and Mystery at the innermost core.

When we list body, mind, and spirit in this order, we do well to remember that this is not the sequence in which we become aware of them. The body as a "physical configuration" needs a mind to become aware at all, and we need the Self—"the Observer"—to become aware that we have a body and a mind. Our actual awareness starts "from the deepest layers up." Pierre Teilhard de Chardin expressed this when he wrote, "We are not human beings having a spiritual experience. We are spiritual beings having a human experience." And yet, it is not in some abstract way but as bodily beings that we have these insights. Can we be aware of our body as embodied Spirit and not treat it with the deep respect it deserves? Learning to live in our body with full awareness increases both our enjoyment of it and our awe for the Mystery it embodies.

BUDDHISM

Among the different aspects of Buddhism in its many forms, this book stresses one above all others: silence. Silence is as basic to Buddhism as Word is to the Amen Traditions and understanding-by-doing is to Hinduism. This refers not only to the "noble silence" of the Buddha—his refusal to answer speculative questions that are not directly related to spiritual practice. For the

Buddha, silence is far more than the refusal to speak. It has above all a positive meaning. In one of his most important sermons the Buddha speaks not a word. He silently lifts up a flower. Only one in the audience understands this famous "Flower Sermon." He proves this by smiling in silence. The Buddha smiled back and, it is said, hands at that moment his tradition on to his smiling successor. That tradition is simply the silence. The Amen Traditions trust in the Word; Buddhism descends into the silence, from which that Word arises.

CHOICE*

COMMITMENT*

COMPREHENSION

Comprehension is the act of grasping an intellectual content through concepts, seizing it, and getting it into our grip. In our culture, this is the usual way of dealing with reality. A closer look, however, shows us that this way of treating the world is rather one-sided and even violent. It leads to isolation: it separates us as subjects from the rest of reality as objects we manipulate. But there is a gentler way available to us, a mutual touch like an embrace, rather than our usual grabbing. We can relate to reality as bridegroom and bride, and so come to understand* rather comprehend it. (See also Mystery)

CONSCIOUSNESS

The distinction between matter and psyche—between our outer and our inner experience—is obvious to all of us. We are not likely to confuse our body with our mind. We do, however, tend to confuse our mind with our consciousness. Mind and psyche are synonyms, but consciousness in the sense of direct awareness is only one manifestation of our psyche; others are thinking, feeling, volition, and so on. Psychological research has discovered a deeper, unconscious layer of our mind of which we are only indirectly aware, which interacts with consciousness through dreams and in many other ways. We disregard its guidance at great risk: "When an inner situation is not made conscious, it appears outside as fate," writes C. G. Jung. Moreover, he discovered, on a still deeper level than our *personal* unconscious, a *collective* unconscious that we share with all human beings and that seems to be part of the human psyche since its beginnings in history. With regard to our reflexive consciousness—our being conscious of being conscious—Jung says, "Consciousness is a late-born descendant of the unconscious psyche."[1]

In fact, consciousness hardly deserves that name, unless it also embraces its unconscious levels. Integrating them within our consciousness is an arduous, lifelong task central to cultivating mindfulness. Concerning that task, Jung says, "There is no coming to consciousness without pain." Speaking of a consciousness that disregards the unconscious is the psychological way of referring to an I that forgets the Self.

We have mind in common with even the most primitive living beings: they show such aspects of the psyche as recognition and volition when they distinguish between food and poison, pursue the one and flee the other. We do not know to what extent even pre-living matter participates in mind, but it would stand to reason that mind and matter are two aspects of being in all its forms. However, we share consciousness only with a few higher animals, and it seems that *reflexive* consciousness is our privilege as human beings—a privilege that implies the responsibility to use it for the good of the whole Earth-Household. (See also Mind, Matter, Mindfulness, Earth Household)

---

[1] C. G. Jung, *Modern Man in Search of a Soul* (New York: Harcourt Brace, 1955), 350.

DEATH

Death and life belong inseparably together. A "good death" is the culmination of a life well lived. It is both our ultimate task and the ultimate gift. After all, in dying we are not passive. You cannot even say that you are "being died." Dying is the activity that sums up all our previous deaths. Rightly understood, we do not die only once at the end of our life, but countless times in the course of it. If we do not let go of everything this moment contains, we cannot be fully alive in the next moment. Letting go is the essence of dying and is a skill we need to practice every day by a fervent belonging without clinging, so that in the end we can let go of life, like a ripe fruit that drops from its tree on a sunny autumn day. Mary Oliver writes,

Look, the trees
are turning
their own bodies
into pillars

of light,
are giving off the rich
fragrance of cinnamon
and fulfillment,

the long tapers
of cattails
are bursting and floating away over
the blue shoulders

of the ponds,
and every pond,
no matter what its
name is, is

nameless now.
Every year
everything
I have ever learned

in my lifetime
leads back to this: the fires
and the black river of loss
whose other side

is salvation,
whose meaning
none of us will ever know.
To live in this world

you must be able
to do three things:
to love what is mortal;
to hold it

against your bones knowing
your own life depends on it;
and, when the time comes to let it go,
to let it go.[2]

"Humans do not die from death, but from fully matured love"
(Otto Mauer). (See also God)

---

[2] Mary Oliver, "In Blackwater Woods," in *Devotions: The Selected Poems of Mary Oliver* (New York: Penguin Books, 2020), 389–90.

DESIRE

Desire has garnered undeserved bad press among spiritual writers, as if all desires were impure. According to its Latin origin, the very word means "relating to a star" or "following a star"—your star. You purify your desires not by suppressing them but by finding your highest star and hitching your heart to it.

DEVELOPMENT

Development is an important concept for finding orientation in life. Under Life,* we have discussed at length its threefold meanings—unfolding, rounding out, and revealing.

DIGNITY

Dignity has to do with worthiness and worth, which are root meanings of this word's Latin origin. Rare things are of higher worth than common ones. How great, then, the dignity of unique things! When we recognize the uniqueness of every being, every event, we go through life with great reverence. As we recognize the dignity of every human being, we become conscious also of our own dignity that does not depend on its recognition by others. Persons who become aware of this gain what we call a spiritual backbone.* They walk upright and do not stoop to what is below their dignity.

DISTINCTION

In order to find our orientation, making careful distinctions is one of the most helpful tasks. In the course of this book, we keep finding necessary though neglected distinctions at every step. Thus, we need to distinguish between I and Myself, purpose and meaning, fear and anxiety, comprehending and understanding, The I/You world and the I/It world, and other such pairs. As urgent as it is to make such distinctions and avoid confusion, it is equally important not to push distinction to the point of separation. A leading thinker, Herbert Pietschmann, coined the motto "Distinguish without separating. Combine without equating." (See also Ego,* Mystery)

DOCTRINE

Doctrine—together with morals* and ritual*—is one component of all religions. It is the intellectual effort to express insights of common human religiousness in the language of a given culture, to make them understandable and convincing to people at the time of the founding of a particular religion. If, at later times, this language becomes incomprehensible, the given religion will try to translate it into a contemporary idiom, so as to keep it understandable and persuasive.

It is of the utmost importance to note that religious insights are always expressed in the language of poetry.* Prose cannot convey the weight of such insights. This characteristic helps us distinguish between religious and scientific statements. When we forget that all language about Mystery is to be taken allegorically, not literally, we can go far astray. Thus, Jewish religious scholar Pinchas Lapide says poignantly, "One can take the Bible seriously or one can take it literally; both together is impossible."[3] This could be said of the holy books of all religions.

DOUBLE REALM

Poet Rainer Maria Rilke coined the term "double realm" originally to express the insight that the domains of the living and the departed are at the same time two and yet one realm—in the

---

[3] Pinchas Lapide, *Ist die Bibel richtig übersetzt?* (Gütersloher: Gütersloher Verlagshaus, 1987), 12. My translation.

sense of *Advaita*, nonduality. In his *Sonnets to Orpheus*, the poet illustrates this double realm by the image of a pond mirroring its surroundings. The concept can be applied to a great variety of phenomena. Wherever a whole is, more correctly speaking, "not-two" rather than "one," we are confronted with this mysterious double realm.

EARTH HOUSEHOLD

Earth Household is an image introduced by the poet Gary Snyder in the title of his 1957 book, *Earth House Hold* (literally translating the term "ecology"). It signaled a dramatic change in the public imagination: from the "Kingdom of Nature"—a power pyramid—to a network of relations in a household. A scientific counterpart is the Gaia hypothesis. Developed in the early 1970s by British chemist James Lovelock, US biologist Lynn Margulis, and others, it proposes that all organisms and their inorganic surroundings on Earth are closely integrated to form a single and self-regulating complex system, comparable to a household, maintaining the conditions for life on the planet. One can hardly overestimate the power of images like Earth Household or Gaia to influence not only the imagination of a society but its way of acting. This applies also to the image of the Great Dance introduced by C. S. Lewis in his space novel *Perelandra* (1943), which we have quoted in this book.

ECOLITERACY

Ecoliteracy is a term coined by physicist Fritjof Capra suggesting that it is no longer enough to be literate in the sense of being able to read and write, but we need to also be current on basic principles of ecology. "Life creates conditions conducive to life" (Alexander Laszlo), and if we want to be in tune with Life, we have to study those conditions and support them by the way we live and stand up in public for protecting nature in all its forms.

One important result of ecoliteracy is biomimicry, the principle of imitating nature in designing our technology and our organizational structures. Nature can teach us how to live in harmony with it and with each other and, thus, to thrive. This principle was powerfully promoted by Janine Benyus.

EGO*

ENTITLEMENT

Entitlement is the unfounded conviction that Life owes me a living. It misses the fact that everything is gift, even my very existence. The more we realize this fact, the more the sense of entitlement will be replaced by a sense of gratitude. This would mark a decisive switch toward a healthy society because gratefulness appreciates and cares for things, for example, the environment, while entitlement's way of taking everything for granted leads to careless use and abuse.

The idea of entitlement is actually based on a very positive insight: the recognition of universal human rights, a most significant step forward in human consciousness. The typical entitlement mentality, however, is an egoistic distortion of the idea of human rights. It springs from a scarcity mentality and from the myopic perception of always receiving less than one deserves. Unfortunately, this mentality is widespread today, feeding a feeling of permanent dissatisfaction. This prevents us from enjoying the many gifts we have received. But it is also the trigger for today's gratitude boom. More and more people are discovering the joy of Grateful Living, as the opposite of that entitlement mentality and as an antidote against the unhappiness it generates.

ENVIRONMENT

Environment means more than surroundings. It implies interaction. It is "the world in which we live" with awareness, and thus it has a different size and content for different living beings, depending on their sense organs and relationships with their surroundings. The world of, say, an earthworm will be more limited than that of a dog. Our human world has become nearly limitless. Because of the incomparable range of our sense organs, now helped by technical instruments, vast ranges of the cosmos—the very large as well as the very small—have become the world in which we live: our environment. With this goes an increase of responsibility.

"Environment" as an abstract term for the world of nature allows us to think of it as something distinct from us. Distinct, yes, but not separate. As soon as we push the distinction to the point of separation, we begin to conceive of the environment merely as our natural surroundings—out there. We think of it as the natural habitat of polar bears, whales, and so on. But it is also our own natural habitat—our home. We need to let the word "home," with its wealth of warm emotions, resonate in our mind as often as we speak of our environment. Like a home, it conditions and influences our health, growth, and progress. We want to make it a warm and loving home for all its many different inhabitants, for "our family" in the widest sense.

We could not survive for one day without a million-fold interactions with our environment, about most of which we are unaware.

ETERNITY

Eternity must not be misunderstood as being endless time. In fact, eternity is the very opposite of time. Time is the passage of future into past. Eternity is "the now that does not pass away," as Saint Augustine defines it.

ETHICS

As we use this term here, ethics is the set of principles and guide-lines that determines responsible attitude and activity. In this definition, the word "responsible" deserves special attention. It implies two roots of ethics: awareness and response—awareness of a claim made on us by life and our response to it.

Thus, ethics springs from recognizing and acknowledging that life is making demands on us and is asking for a response. We can also become aware that life has a direction: it wants, for instance, diversity, the well-being of all its members, and their free unfold-ing in interaction with all others. We can trust this flow of life, letting it guide us and adjusting our actions to it. This constitutes ethical behavior.

Understood in this way, ethics is responsible behavior, our positive response to life's demands—our "yes!" to life. Irrespon-sible behavior, in contrast, results from our "no" that resists the direction of life—for example, out of mismanaged anxiety, short-sighted greed, or impatience. This no is called fear. From the yes of trust springs ethical behavior; from the no of fear, unethical behavior.

Ethics Are More Important Than Religion reads the challeng-ing title of the Dalai Lama's appeal to humanity, a clarion call for which the time is ripe. It would be reckless to ignore the voice of this sage. "We are not born members of a particular religion," says the Dalai Lama, "but ethics are innate to us." Yes, indeed! And why innate? Because ethics is inseparably part of our religious-ness, our consciousness of the Great Mystery. That consciousness is innate to us and even characterizes us as human beings. What the Dalai Lama calls ethics is an essential aspect of that religious-ness, of our grappling with Mystery. Thus, we can completely agree with his statement and express it in our terms by saying, "Religiousness is more important than the religions," which are its expressions in history.

Ethics is the positive response to the demand Mystery makes on us: our yes to the Mystery of life. (See Religiousness)

EVIL

In order to extricate the concept of evil from debatable moral definitions, we prefer to speak not of good and evil but replace those two terms with "life-affirming" and "life-denying."

As life-*denying*, "evil" is essentially a lack. Lack isn't something, but the *absence* of something: "the no of all nothing," as E. E. Cummings calls it. Yet, in practice, mere lack can cause great harm.

We have basically two choices of viewing that terrible negative power we call evil. We can either look at it with the eyes of the proverbial knight in white armor, or with the eyes of a mother who without underestimating evil sees it as the not-yet-good. Experience shows that fighting evil, no matter how idealistically, leads to greater evil. But motherly eyes have a power of their own. And they empower the wayward child to recover the always present core of goodness deep within us by the very compassion of their glance.

FAITH*

FEAR

Fear needs to be distinguished from fright. When we perceive a danger, we cannot help getting frightened, but we need not react fearfully; we can train ourselves to respond with courage. In a courageous response to any threat, we acknowledge being frightened but face the danger and mobilize all our energy to overcome it. Courage is so obviously the appropriate response that it is hard to explain why we so often react fearfully, why we typically resent rather than face the danger, and why we waste our energy in blaming someone, maybe Life itself, for treating us that way. We have our own ideas of what we "deserve," and this entitlement mentality is based on wishful thinking rather than on realistic trust.

The opposite of fear is trust—not, however, trust in our own limited strength and insight, but trust in life.

FREEDOM

When we think about freedom, we tend to focus on what hinders us from acting freely. But it may be helpful to start by distinguishing between "freedom from" and "freedom for."

What do we want to use our freedom for? Whatever your answer may be, you will name something that contributes to your full, unhampered development. Do we know, however, what we need for our development? We do not even know it at the biological level. In fact, we have to rely on life. Life develops and maintains our body through countless processes of which we are, for the most part unaware. Thus, if free development is our goal, we will do well to trust life more than our own ideas and plans. What truly makes us free is a thorough listening to the guidance of life moment by moment and "guidance" in this sense means the way fine dancers lead their partners.

This shows us that "freedom from" refers primarily to everything that hinders us to trust in the guidance of life. External circumstances, no matter how limiting they may appear to our sense of freedom, are nevertheless gifts of Life, and Life always has our full and healthy development for its goal. If the goal of "freedom for" is self-development through trust in life, "freedom from" must focus on the inner obstacles against that trust: fear.

A convincing example is the fearless attitude of Viktor Frankl. In his book *Yes to Life: In Spite of Everything*, he proves from his own concentration camp experience that a human being can remain free, despite the most horrible external constraints by trusting the guidance of Life.

FRUGALITY

This word has a much richer meaning than we tend to give to it. Many people use "frugal" to mean merely "thrifty" or "economical," in a sense that tends to slide over into skimpy, if not outright miserly. This negative connotation is promoted by an exploitative economy, based on manipulating customers into spending money on what they do not need. In opposition to this trend, frugal people choose their lifestyle according to their own values and ideals. Frugal living means intentional living—awake, alert, and oriented toward goals of one's own choice.

As a frugal shopper, you may, for instance, choose clothes that are less fashionable but of higher quality, or buy equipment that costs somewhat more, because it is solidly built and will last longer. You will look for quality rather than quantity. Above all, you will ask yourself the central question of frugal living: how much is enough? This question is rightly considered subversive by our corrupt economy. The more people ask, "How much is enough?" and act accordingly, the closer we are to healing not only our economy but our whole planet.

Our English word "frugal" comes from Latin *frux*, meaning fruit in the wider sense of fruit and vegetables. This gives the term overtones of vegetarian and vegan living. Until recently, most people lived on farms, where homegrown produce was their daily fare, meat being reserved for special occasions. In this context, frugal living meant a household living with proud self-sufficiency within its means—gratefully and joyfully. Applied to the whole world-household today, everything but vegan living is beyond our means. The sooner we, as the human family, learn to live frugally in this full sense of the word, the better for us and for generations to come.

A simple test of grateful living is the answer to the question "Do I just want this, or do I really need it?" Let us not forget, however, that beauty is not a mere want but one of our genuine needs. The most gratifying beauty, however, is the beauty of frugality.

I had only two copper coins.
For one I bought bread,
For the other daffodils.

(Source unknown)

GIVE-AND-TAKE

All life processes involve a mutual give-and-take. This is as true in psychology as it is in biology. Too often we think of "give-and-take" only as a principle governing fair compromise in negotiations, but this is far too restrictive a view. Giving and taking are two all-pervading ways of acting. To keep them in balance is a primary prerequisite for a well-balanced life. We have referred to this task mostly implicitly in the context of finding orientation, hence a few explicit considerations here.

Taking is a characteristic activity of the *animus* in Jungian terms; giving is more typical for the *anima*. Just as a healthy animus/anima integration is necessary for a healthy personality, so is finding the right integration between giving and taking. You can check for yourself how far our prevailing mentality is out of balance in this respect: you need only keep track of how often you say, "I take," compared to, "I give." You take a walk, take a meal, a shower, a ride, a left turn, a right.... And how often do you find yourself saying, "I give"? Hardly more often, I bet, than you say "I don't give a——!" We even grotesquely claim that we "take" things that no one can take: how do you "*take* a nap"? As long as you insist on *taking* that nap, you'll surely stay awake; you'll have to *give* yourself to it—"let yourself sink into the arms of sleep," as they said in antiquity—in order to fall asleep.

Giving and taking mark two opposite attitudes that need to be balanced in all areas of daily life. Think only of the expression "I'll *take* a look." What an imbalanced way of looking! We can learn with "soft eyes" to "give a look" while taking one. Then our looking at things will not be a taking possession of them, but a mutual embrace, as of bridegroom and bride. Generalizing, we can say that the give-and-take approach to life is an approach with love, a "yes" to mutual belonging. (See also Comprehension)

God

A special section in part 1 deals with this keyword. The main point of our approach is that we use "God" as a synonym for "Mystery" when we want to emphasize human *interaction* with that Ultimate Reality. Mystery is for theists, atheists, and agnostics alike the unfathomable Ground of being. Agnostics leaves it at that. Theists go a step further and explore their relationship to that Great Mystery—which they call God—through worship, prayer, meditation, and the lifelong adventure of faith and trust. Atheists object to theistic forms of interaction with Mystery, but they may have their own forms—often not even recognizing them as such—for instance, a deep ethical commitment.

God, in this sense, is not an invention of religious imagination, like the gods, but a discovery—the central discovery of our innate religiousness. Domestication of our notion of God through mixing it up with some aspects of the gods remains a constant hazard. That is why, in this book, we prefer to speak of "Mystery," when we mean, in G. M. Hopkins's lapidary phrase, "past all grasp God." (See also Ethics, Mystery, Religiousness, Trust*)

Good/Bad

The word "good" inevitably raises questions—regarding the point of view, the area of application, the standard applied.

Good—from whose point of view? What is good news for one team is bad news for their opponents. For fruit flies a rotten apple is a good apple. It all depends on the point of view.

Good—in what respect? That a teacher is good does not necessarily mean that he is good as a driver, a fly-fisher, or even as a human being. We need to consider the area to which the word "good" applies.

Good—by what standards? The range of precision that is good, when measuring the temperature of stars, is not good enough when measuring your body temperature. What "good" means actually depends on our standard of evaluation.

When using "good" in this book, we want to include as many points of view as possible (and not only those of humans). We want to make the area to which the word "good" applies as comprehensive as we can, and our standard of evaluation as widely applicable as possible. In order to fulfill these conditions, "good," when not otherwise indicated, here means "life-affirming." This allows us to avoid the terms "bad" or "evil" altogether and say instead, "life-denying" or "life-destroying." Thus, we can bypass fruitless moral controversies and anchor our understanding of so-called good and evil* not in the moral* conventions of this or that society, but in the common ground of ethics* that all human beings share.

For all practical purposes, it is sufficient to cultivate a thorough listening with the ears of the heart, which is obedience to Life. This takes us in the direction of all that is called "good." In contrast, obdurate resistance to Life and its demands brings about all that is called "bad." Keeping this in mind will go a long way in saving us from getting ensnared in theories, and rather helping us find our orientation in life.

Grateful Living*

Happiness

Happiness, as usually understood, depends on chance occurrences. It is good fortune that makes us happy, and that comes by sheer good luck. However, "Luck has a way of evaporating when you lean on it" (Brandon Mull), and we want a happiness we can lean on. The human heart desires happiness that lasts. Is this a wishful dream, or does harsh reality admit of lasting happiness? It does indeed. Joy* is lasting happiness, a happiness that does not depend on what happens. And the key to joy is gratefulness.

Even when the worst things happen to us, we can remain joyful, as long as we remain grateful for the new opportunities that misfortune brings with it—opportunities to grow by the painful experience; to learn courage, patience, and tenacity; to toughen up, to stand our ground. All these opportunities, no matter how demanding, are gifts for which we can be grateful. And as long as we remain grateful, we remain cheerful, upbeat, and content even amid misfortune. Through gratefulness we feel a deep joy in spite of suffering because we trust that Life knows best what we need at any given moment. Lasting happiness can lean on our trust. Then and there, that trust may seem to be blind faith, but in retrospect, trust in Life always proves justified.

Looking at it from a different angle, Eliyahu Goldratt said, "Good luck is when opportunity meets preparation, while bad luck is when lack of preparation meets reality." The most essential preparation for opportunity is trust in life. When opportunity meets that preparation, it leads to more than mere good luck; it sparks genuine, lasting happiness.

HEART

Heart is the symbol for the innermost core of anything—*cor* being the Latin word for heart—as in the heart of lettuce, the heart of a city, or the heart of a teacher's message. Applied to humans, too, heart means the innermost realm of our being, as in the phrase "I was pouring out my heart to a friend." Standing for the essence, heart stands for our being as a whole—body and spirit; thinking, feeling, willing, nothing must be excluded.

Too often we overemphasize the emotions when we speak of the heart. This one-sided emphasis can lead to grave misunderstandings. Thus, following a "path with heart" means a great deal more than being driven by your emotions. Since the heart stands for the whole, it also includes all that we mean by "brain."

Following the "path with heart" implies responsibility. The difference between *flowing* with Life and *responding* to Life is the difference between a log drifting down the river and a fish swimming by responding most sensitively to the river's currents. Because "heart" means our innermost being, it is also the realm of our deepest relationships—as when we speak "heart to heart" with one another or even say that we are "one heart." As bridgehead of all relationships, the heart is also our point of encounter with the Great Mystery. (See Religiousness, Ethics)

HINDUISM

We are limiting ourselves here to a most highly simplified presentation of the relationships between the world's three great spiritual traditions. Under this perspective, *silence* is at the heart of Buddhism, *word* at the heart of the Amen Traditions, and *understanding-by-doing* at the heart of Hinduism. We understand a word when we listen so deeply to it that it takes hold of us, inspires us to act in response to it, and so leads us back to its source, the silence. Only through this obedient doing can we truly understand. All forms of Yoga* are variations of understanding-by-doing. Swami Venkatesananda says succinctly, "Yoga is understanding."

HOLY

The words "holy," "whole," and "healthy" spring from the same root in the English language. Holy means healthy and whole through a healing relationship to the Great Mystery. The "holy ones" are people who orientate their lives by having the Great

Mystery as the ultimate reference point. They create a culture in which everything is hallowed through becoming transparent for Mystery—for example, holy places or a sacred season. The more mindfully we live, the more clearly we see the relationship to the Great Mystery that makes everything holy. That is why St. Benedict writes in his rule for monks that they should handle every pot and pan in the monastery with the same reverence as the sacred vessels on the altar. When we extend this principle to all aspects of everyday living, our daily life becomes more and more holy and healthy.

HOPE

Hope in the full spiritual sense of the word means something quite different from "hope" in everyday language. What we hope for in everyday life is always something we can imagine, but hope in the spiritual sense is openness for the unimaginable, openness for surprise. That is why we need to watch out; our hopes can even get in the way of genuine hope if we cling to what we can imagine and fail to trust that life knows better.

HUMAN DIGNITY

Under dignity* we consider that basic dignity to which every human being is entitled. Unfortunately, many people are not aware of their dignity. To grow into consciousness of his or her human dignity, a child needs two things: being loved unconditionally and being recognized, affirmed, and supported in its uniqueness. Because so many children today lack these two essential experiences, more and more people are feeling worthless and degraded. For adults it is difficult to make up for what they were not given in childhood. However, even adults who are in this way underprivileged can come to the insight that life gives them what they need to become aware of their dignity, even if their parents and caregivers failed to do so. We stand in the great network* of life and belong unconditionally to that great community. Not only that, but life loves us and affirms us in our uniqueness. We can rely on that. There never was nor will be another human being like you, and life says yes to you just as you are.

Human dignity—our own and that of every human being—deserves top priority as subject matter in basic education today. But the misery in our world makes it almost impossible for some people to feel loved and recognized. Extreme poverty is thus a crime against human dignity and poses a most urgent challenge to the whole human family. Misery can be overcome, and according to reliable experts, this goal is within realistic reach. Each one of us needs to find a place in this enterprise and go to work without delay. Our own human dignity demands it.

I*

INNER-OUTER*

INSIGHT

Insight results from the encounter of our reason with reality. Something external affects our inner awareness, but at the same time, our awareness takes hold in its own way of what it perceives. Through this mutual interaction, something new results: we gain insight into something that acts on its own and is not simply invented by us. Our insight takes hold of it without taking away its autonomy. Two realms are interacting here: inner and outer. Dissolving one into the other would not do justice to the fact that we receive something new. Doubting this basic experience leads to denying that we can ever gain reliable insight. Trusting this basic experience, we can gain ever-new insights on a realistic basis.

INSTITUTIONS

Institutions are a form of organization created for the benefit of individuals, the general public, or both. Once an organically grown community concerned with a particular field of activities reaches a certain size, it needs an institutional structure for its functioning and further development. There is nothing wrong with that. However, we must not overlook the danger that is inevitably connected with institutionalization. Experience shows that institutions take on a life of their own and have the tendency to increasingly neglect their original purpose and put most of their energy into self-perpetuation. Anyone can observe this in political, academic, medical, and many other institutions.

For our orientation, it is important to realize that the same tendency to become self-centered and self-serving is also present in religious institutions. We need to keep this danger in mind and try to forestall it. Institutions are a necessary evil, but since they are necessary, we need to learn to make the most positive use of them. Members of religious institutions can soberly face this fact, try to minimize the negative tendencies, and reorient them again and again toward the primal goal: to foster the encounter with Mystery.

IT*

JOY

Joy is the happiness* for which the human heart longs, a lasting happiness, a happiness that does not depend on what happens. Unhappiness always results from wanting one thing while Life is giving us something different. Thus, the royal road to joy is trust that Life knows better than we ourselves what is good for us. The implications of this basic principle are manifold and far-reaching. Yet just being aware of the principle will go a long way to help us in our efforts at orientation.

LEISURE

Leisure is not the privilege of people who can afford to take time off, but the virtue of people who give time to what takes time—as much time as it deserves. In doing so, they are in tune with the rhythm of life.

German philosopher Josef Pieper made a convincing case in his book *Leisure: The Basis of Culture.* A flourishing culture owes its creation as much to play as to work. In our personal lives, too, leisure makes room for creativity, enjoyment, and celebration, for all that is most important to us. But we live in a culture that is so work- and achievement-oriented that it makes us feel guilty when we take time for leisure. In this respect, we need to take a countercultural stance. In fact, we will be truly creative only when we perform even our work leisurely—more playfully.

LIFE*

LILA

Lila is a Sanskrit word meaning "play." In Hinduism, *lila* refers to the idea that we can ultimately recognize in all that happens the Great Mystery at play—the Great Sacred Dance of the universe. Not only for Hindus but for all of us, this image is worth pondering. The meaning of our life, we may discover, is learning to stay in step with the cosmic dance.

LOVE

Love is more than a feeling. It is an attitude that involves all realms of a person's being. In fact, the emotional aspect is not necessarily predominant. Yes, when we "fall in love," we experience a strong sense of benevolence. But when we rise to the challenge of "loving our enemies," we do not spontaneously *feel* that love.

There are so many kinds of love that it seems almost hopeless to find a definition that will cover them all. Mother love, romantic love, love of our pets, of our country, of God . . . It took me a long time to find a common denominator for all forms of love. Whenever we love, we say an unlimited benevolent yes to belonging. Love is the lived yes to mutual belonging. (See also God)

MAGIC

Strictly speaking, magic differs from religiosity* in one decisive point. Both are dealing with the Great Mystery, but magic tries to find ways of manipulating Mystery, while religiosity attempts to find what the Mystery "wants" and do it obediently. The word "magic" is also used with a positive meaning—for instance, when we speak of a "magic moment." Behind this more superficial usage stands the image of a magician who can fulfill our wishes by conjuring up surprising effects.

MATTER

Matter originally means the material, the stuff of which everything consists—in contrast to its immaterial aspect, which we call mind. "Matter" and "mother" come from the same linguistic root. As we find our orientation in the universe, we learn to love matter as the dark motherly soil in which we are rooted and honor mind as the clear light toward which we are growing. To call them two "realities" is not quite accurate. The term fits only material reality, for it implies "thingness"—*realitas* from *res*, in Latin. "Actualities" sounds a bit awkward, but it could be used as an overarching term for mind and matter, since both do *act*, though in very different ways.

The fact that we need our mind to be aware of matter in the first place shows that mind cannot be reduced to an "epiphenomenon" of matter. However, the clear distinction between the two must not be pushed to the point of separating them. They may be understood as interrelated aspects of what C. G. Jung and W. Pauli called "unus mundis," the One World. Already in the nineteenth century, Gustav Fechner and Wilhelm Wundt spoke of two perspectives: matter seen from the inside is mind; mind seen from the outside is matter. (See also Mind)

MEANING/PURPOSE

In everyday speech, we tend to use the words "meaning" and "purpose" interchangeably. Such careless speaking can lead us to muddled thinking and, in turn, to unfocused doing. Therefore, a more precise use of the terms is important for our orientation.

Purpose relates to work; meaning, to play. We work in order to achieve a purpose, but playing is meaningful, without aiming at any purpose beyond itself. As soon as work achieves its purpose, it comes to an end; to continue would be meaningless. But play can go on and on; it is meaningful in itself.

To achieve a well-balanced life, we need to balance purpose and meaning. But we will not reach this goal by jumping back and forth from working to playing. We need to integrate the two—to do our work, whatever it may be, with a playful attitude. Any work that you can perform with full presence and with the intention of serving others will be meaningful and, in this sense, playful and worth doing for its own sake. If, considering all this, we ask for the meaning of life, we find a highly surprising answer: a meaningful life must be a playful life. Hinduism speaks of *lila**— the Great Mystery playing in us and through us. We have called it the Great Dance. (See Mystery)

MIND

The English word "mind" originally meant "memory," but this connotation was gradually extended, and now "mind" designates all of the psyche as distinct from matter. The distinction between mind and matter is an experiential fact: no matter how complete an explanation of physical phenomena, it cannot explain our subjective consciousness of these phenomena. Clarifying the relationship between the two has been called "the hard problem" of consciousness; science,* within its self-set limits, is not equipped to solve it.

In our search for orientation, it will be helpful to remember that reducing mind to matter, or matter to mind, fails to do justice to their distinct characteristics. Yet pushing their distinction to the point of separation fails to acknowledge their interdependence. We need our embodied mind to investigate matter; mental activity, in turn, presupposes material structures (the brain).

Mind causes changes in our body—as when a thought makes us blush; the body in turn affects the mind—as when we get drunk. We may think of mind and matter as two distinct but inseparable aspects of one integral conscious existence. (See Body, Matter)

MINDFULNESS

In everyday language, mindfulness means an intense conscious awareness of something, a state of attention characterized by fully focusing our mind on it. This mental process typically narrows the focus of our attention—as when the area on which we focus a magnifying glass gets smaller as it gets sharper. In contrast, mindfulness—in the language of spiritual practice—refers to an attention through which the focus widens as it gets sharper. "Concentration without elimination," T. S. Eliot calls this paradox. Mindfulness in this sense focuses on the present moment with all it contains within wider and wider horizons and in ever greater depth.

The mainspring of every spiritual practice is mindfulness. Today's mindfulness practices are typically therapeutic techniques that teach us to acknowledge and accept our feelings, thoughts, desires, and bodily sensations. This runs a risk: it can easily turn into an excessive preoccupation with ourselves that neglects the wide network of relationships in which we find ourselves. Grateful living as a mindfulness practice is safe from this trap because it always implies relationship. Gratitude is "interactive mindfulness."

Morals

Morals—together with doctrine* and ritual*—are one component of all religions. In this sense, morals denote the effort of
the human will (in the sense of willingness) to express the ethics of common human religiousness in the language of a given
culture, to make them understandable and convincing to people
at the time when that particular religion is being founded. If, in
the course of history, the cultural conditions change significantly,
that religious tradition will have to try to deal with newly arising
moral problems and adjust its moral code in order to assure that
it will remain a lighthouse in which ethics is the lantern.

In the same way as religiousness finds expression in religions,
ethics finds expression in morals. Ethics, in this sense, is responsibility—ultimately the conscientious use of our ability to respond
to the Mystery of Life. Morals represent the attempt to apply ethics to the whole network of relations in a given culture.

In a less specialized sense, morals are simply the rules of
behavior acknowledged by a given social group. In essence,
every moral code in the world has always said, "This is how one
behaves when one belongs to us." In the course of history, this
"us" grew from the smallest circle of an extended family or a tribe
to include wider and wider circles. By now, it must be all-inclusive,
or it can no longer claim to be moral. Today's morals must be
built on the fact that all of us belong together: not only humans,
of course, but animals, plants, and our whole environment. (See
also Ethics, Religiousness)

Mystery

Whenever Mystery or the Great Mystery is mentioned in these
pages, remember that this does not refer to something vague or
mystifying, but to something we encounter at every turn, with a
minimum of mindfulness. Mystery is a power that affects us and

everything there is, yet we cannot *grasp* it intellectually. We can, however, understand it to the extent to which we interact with it from our heart. (See also Heart, Distinction)

MYSTIC

A mystic is a person who has mystic experiences—someone who becomes blissfully aware that ultimately all is one. This happens in our peak experiences*: we feel the surpassing joy of all-oneness. In this respect, the mystic is not a special kind of human being, but every human being is a special kind of mystic. What, then, distinguishes the ones we call the great mystics? They let this mystic realization flow into every aspect of their lives. This is what our peak experiences challenge us to become: people who consciously live in touch with mystery and let it determine the shape of their daily life. (See Mystery)

NAME

Webster's Dictionary defines "name" as "a word or set of words by which a person or thing is known, addressed, or referred to." That we *refer* to people or things by their name and *address* them by that name is a matter of daily experience. In this respect, one's name or nickname is a "handle," in the sense of a username on a social media website. In the Grimms' fairytale, one gains magic power over the little straw-spinning imp by being able to address him as Rumpelstiltskin. When you can name one of your evasive emotions, or even a dog, you have the feeling of gaining some control over it. In *addressing* and *referring* to something or someone, a name is useful. But when it comes to *knowing* we need to be aware that any name affords merely the most superficial kind of knowledge.

Names are labels for people and things, but one's name—in the full sense of the word—is more than a label. Always in the singular, name stands for that evasive phenomenon underneath all labels, to which names are affixed in an attempt to identify it. But identification always falls short of grasping identity. Raimon Panikkar made this important distinction between identity and identification. We identify ourselves by our names, but our Name is our true identity, which defies identification. Not even we ourselves know our true Name—for two reasons: it is still in the state of becoming and it is ultimately hidden in mystery.

Our name—who we are—grows and changes throughout life, with every new experience. That is why Rumi can say, "No one will know my true Name, until my last breath goes out." But we may ask, will anyone know it, even then? There is so much more to our life than our biography. We can only tell what we can take hold of, but in our best and most important moments, Life takes hold of us instead—in our peak moments, when we experience our one-ness with all there is and with Mystery as its essence. When that happens, we lose all labels and names, only our naked Name remains. From now on, *all* names will be *our* names, because each of them points toward the *one* Name. In his famous poem "Call me by my true names," Thich Nhat Hanh suggests that all names are, in truth, everyone's names, because we are all one.

We are one in Mystery, we share *the* Name par excellence. But that name is ineffable. That is why names given to God in the Jewish tradition are never pronounced but replaced by *ha shem*— "*the* Name." If we keep this in mind, we will treat all names with reverence, remembering that an unspeakable depth lies behind them. We will pronounce names with respect for the unnamable to which they refer. A name can be a "handle" only in the sense of opening a door that leads ultimately into Mystery.

NETWORK

"Nature's basic form of organization is the network." Physicist Fritjof Capra has amply demonstrated this in his books. He has also shown that social structures that do not follow nature's basic network model run the risk of endangering and injuring Life. Proof for this is the power pyramid*—the very opposite of a network—that has become the basic model of our social order. The destructive consequences of our unnatural form of interacting with each other show themselves all too clearly today, both in our social ills and in the environmental damage we are causing. Our very survival depends on a switch to the network as the future form of society. Our orientation in the world calls for network-thinking and network-living as its framework.

The basic difference between a pyramid and a network as social structures is the difference between "Rule from above" and "Rule from below." It concerns the flow of power. In the pyramid, power flows from the top down in a descending chain of command; in the network, power flows from the bottom upward in an ascending chain of empowerment. Here, every decision is made on the lowest level capable of making it—that is to say, by the people directly affected by its consequences. They will empower higher decision-making levels only to the extent to which a decision affects them also—and so on upward through a network of networks in mutual trust.

Nature as a whole is a network of networks, and human networking is the consequence of trusting that "nature knows best." Mutual trust and trust in nature spring from the basic attitude of trust in life.* We survive only because we are embedded in numberless networks. Becoming aware of them allows us to live relaxed and at the same time take responsibility for the cultivation of network structures. One of our primary tasks in life is to cultivate our personal network of relationships.

As individuals we can contribute within our small circle of influence to this worldwide paradigm shift from pyramid to network. Social media and the internet offer great opportunities in this respect but also show the need for discrimination in networking. Becoming aware of the momentous shift that is taking place and staying informed about its development is a necessary task today. Above all, we need to use our power—we have more influence than we think—to empower all with whom we are connected through various networks in daily life.

OBEDIENCE

Obedience means a great deal more than doing what you are told to do. Any dog can learn that in obedience school. Human obedience in the full sense of the word is a deep listening with the heart and a willingness to respond. According to its Latin root, the word obedience (from *ob-audire*) means intensive listening, ultimately a loving listening to Life itself. At any moment, Life tells us something and demands something from us. Even inanimate things "speak" to us in this way. They tell us something about themselves and expect something from us: they want us to treat them carefully and respectfully, mindful of the network of relationships through which they connect us with all other things and with the ground of all things, the Great Mystery.

Obedient listening presupposes that we grow silent. Inner silence can be learned through practice. Out of a silent heart arises quite spontaneously obedient listening. (See Mystery)

OPPORTUNITY

Opportunity is any situation in which we find ourselves, if we consider it under a particular aspect—under the aspect of all that Life is offering us at that moment. In fact, at every moment, life invites us to avail ourselves of ever-new possibilities at hand, and we can choose which ones to make come true. Unfortunately, like sleepwalkers, we tend not to listen, or if we do, we prefer our own agenda. However, life is so generous that even if we miss a given opportunity, life's abundance offers us, at the next moment, another opportunity. And this, again and again, inexhaustibly.

ORIENTATION*

PEAK EXPERIENCE

Peak experience is the name that Abraham Maslow gave to high points—peaks—of human awareness. Those are moments in which we experience ourselves suddenly and blissfully as being inseparably one with all. We cannot put these experiences into words—they are ineffable—but we know the attempts of mystics to write about them, most often in poetic terms. Maslow's research suggests that *every* healthy human being does occasionally have peak experiences—more frequently in childhood and youth—but that we tend to overlook or even suppress them in our memory. Not so for the great mystics. They allow the awareness of all-oneness to shape their whole life.

Maslow was able to prove that, in our peak experiences, the great values—beauty, truth, goodness—become tangible realities to us. Thus, like the great mystics, we too can live in the awareness that we are one with all and make those values the driving forces of our daily lives. In fact, mystics are not a different kind of human being, but every human being is a different kind of mystic.

Peak experiences are always unexpected gifts of life. We cannot force them. We can only prepare ourselves by practicing that inner silence, in which we are more apt to hear these special words of life. Greediness for special experiences is a constant danger for spiritual seekers. Instead, we can cultivate gratitude for what has already been given to us and live by it.

PERFECTION

Perfection is a word we readily understand but also tend to misunderstand. The misunderstanding turns perfection into something static. We may be thinking of the static beauty of a perfect piece of sculpture. But does that sculpture "have" that perfection before the observer discovers it in a dynamic process? To understand perfection in its true sense, we must keep in mind the fullness of interactions that belong to it.

Our perfection does not consist in reaching the top of a static standard but entering the dynamic fullness of which we are capable. It is a matter not of isolated achievement but of full interaction. Its prototype is the dynamic of that perfect "dancing" we observe in nature.

PLAY (SEE MEANING/PURPOSE)

POETRY

The term "poetry" comes from the Greek word *poein* and means simply "to make"—deliberately to create something out of words, namely the poem. It is the poet's deliberate action that is emphasized when we speak of poetry. But as in every act of creating, the raw material is of greatest importance. A woodworker makes a reality out of the possibilities that are latent in his raw material, the wood. The poet allows the latent powers of language to unfold fully. We could use an image and say, language is pregnant with insights waiting for the poet who, like a midwife, helps them come to birth.

Through no other way of speaking can we reach the depth of insight that poetry reveals. That is why we need to use poetry whenever we approach the nearly ineffable.

Poetry demands not only a deliberate way of speaking but also a special way of listening, for which we can train our ears and hearts. The heart of all reveals itself only to a listening heart. "Heart speaks to heart," says St. Augustine. About the insights that poetry offers to our hearts, the fox tells the little prince in the well-known book of Antoine de Saint Exupéry, "Only with the heart does one see clearly. What is essential remains invisible to the eyes." Poetry is the language of the wide-awake heart, a language awed by the enchantment deep down things.

Deep down all things a song is sleeping,
Dreaming, since the dawn of time.
But the world will wake up singing
If you find the magic rhyme.

(Joseph von Eichendorff)

POWER

Power has two aspects: force and influence. All of us exercise power over others, even though we are usually quite unaware of it. Whether we want it or not, we influence and are being influenced by everyone with whom we come in contact. It is helpful to become aware of our power and to live up to the responsibility this implies. Life gives us power so that we can empower others. Power that does not empower those under its influence turns into violence.

In our context of finding orientation, it is *social* power that concerns us. Webster's Dictionary defines it as "possession of control, authority, or influence over others." This definition shows the all-pervasive misconception of power in our sick society: it stresses control and influence "*over* others"—much in the sense of a hierarchical power pyramid—and does not even hint at the possibility that power may be used for others—in their service. Yet in a healthy society, the need for power to constrain others will be an exception; its normal use will be for their empowerment.

A peaceful society encourages in its members a feeling of belonging and of being appreciated—the two pillars on which a sense of human dignity rests. People who grow up in an atmosphere of human dignity typically use their innate powers creatively for the benefit of all. Destructive use of power can frequently be traced to a missing sense of self-worth. Through the example we give to others, each of us is wielding power of which we are rarely aware. We can learn consciously to empower others by giving them a sense of belonging and by sincerely valuing their special talents. Since everything hangs together with everything, we may be sure that our personal attitude will have an influence on the way society as a whole uses power.

To most people an awareness of their power gives pleasure. This sense of pleasure needs to be counterbalanced by a sense of responsibility, in order to avoid a greedy grabbing for power and its detrimental consequences. The weaker our self-assurance, the stronger the temptation to abuse our power over others. Insecurity tends to make the ego power-hungry. The stronger we are founded in our Self, and thus more aware of our dignity as human beings, the easier it will be to respect the human dignity of others and to use our power to foster their well-being.

For a long time, our egocentric attitude as human beings has made us abuse our power over animals, plants, and nature in general, by oppressing and exploiting them. We need to become aware of our intimate interrelatedness with all other beings, and so find ways of using our power in a new, fruitful symbiosis with our natural environment.

POWER PYRAMID

Civilization, as we know it from the last six thousand years, has been driven by fear. This expresses itself in the structure of a pyramid. The most powerful sit at the top and fear being toppled. Out of that fear, they defend their position by any means, violently if necessary. The less powerful fear that others may get ahead of them, and therefore fight with their rivals for higher positions in the pyramid. All of them fear that there is not enough to go around and greedily attempt to amass as much as possible of the available resources. Thus, fear accounts for the dog-eat-dog competition so typical of our society.

The power pyramid fulfilled a certain transitional task in the evolution of society. It provided a framework for organizing coordinated work by large numbers of people, and so it led to some significant social improvements. Yet the built-in fear and violence of the power pyramid have led society to the point of self-destruction. In answer to this threat, countless social networks are springing up all over the world, and the ideal of "imitating nature" is rapidly gaining ground in a variety of fields. Today we need an altogether different social structure, based not on fear but on trust: the network.

PURPOSE (SEE MEANING/PURPOSE)

RELATIONSHIP

Each one of us has been born into a network of relationships—both physiological and social—without which we could not survive. Our development into a fully mature person is determined by the multiplicity, diversity, durability, and depth of relationships that we consciously cultivate. Out of relationships emerges something new—the network—that is more than the sum total of its links.

When we reflect on relationships between people, we usually start with single individuals and proceed by linking them to one another. But how can we think of a hand or an eye isolated from the body? Individuals become what they are only through their relationships. The correct starting point for reflecting on relationships is this mutual linkage. Looking at the big picture, relationship is not a contingent aspect of the whole but its basic given.

RELIGION*

RELIGIOUSNESS*

Religiousness* is our innate sense for Mystery. We might imagine religiousness as the magnetic north that sets the compass needle of our heart—intellect, will, and emotions—toward what we most highly value and desire. For our intellect, that means finding an ultimately reliable basis for deciding what is "really real." This painful search reaches its goal, when the intellect comes to understand Mystery as "Ground of being, and granite of it: past all / Grasp" (G. M. Hopkins, "The Wreck of the Deutschland").

What our will—our willingness, in contrast to our willfulness—desires most profoundly is to be freed from wavering and to be able to make right and just decisions. This, too, can be gained through encounter with Mystery, an encounter triggered for Eichendorff by the awe-inspiring "roar of a storm in the trees of the woods" together with ominous "sheet lightning on the horizon." In a poem that defies translation, this thunderstorm becomes a peak experience for the poet. "It frees his mind" from indecision, as, in a flash, "he recognizes and commits himself ecstatically to all that is authentic, upright, and lofty." What happens in such moments? Mystery appears as a limitless yes that affirms all being, our own included. It calls forth from us in return a spontaneous, irresistible yes that overflows into daily life and makes us relate to everything with love—with a limitless yes to mutual belonging.

Our emotions, too, find fulfillment in the encounter with Mystery. As we saw, the intellect did so under the aspect of truth, the will under the aspect of goodness, and the emotions will do so under the aspect of beauty. In peak experiences we can become aware of mystery as overwhelmingly beautiful—certainly not pretty, but fiercely fascinating. Rilke knew the reason why, when he wrote, "Beauty is but the edge of the dreadful which we can barely survive / and we admire it so, since it serenely distains / just to destroy us." Beauty as the shining edge of ultimate reality is an experience that goes as far back in history and prehistory as cognitive archaeology can find traces of spirituality, for instance, through analysis of cave paintings and other prehistoric art.

Hopkins, Eichendorff, Rilke—we have given the word to three great poets here. It is not by chance that we resort to poetry as often as we try to speak about Mystery. Poetry is the only way—paradoxically—to speak about the unspeakable. (See also Peak Experience, Poetry)

RESPONSIBILITY

Responsibility is, as the word clearly suggests, the ability to respond to a word or a call. But since, as human beings, we have this ability, responsibility also implies our obligation to respond. These are two different meanings.

The central significance of responsibility comes into focus when we realize that everything that happens in a given moment may be understood as a word that life itself addresses to us, expecting our reply. When a child is born to us, it is easy to see that life is speaking to us through this event, setting in motion a process to which we will have to give a great many different answers. Or when a friend is in danger, we obviously have the responsibility to do what life is asking from us at that moment.

This holds true also in less dramatic situations. In fact, at every moment of our daily lives we are invited to play with Life this game of call and answer—a most serious game, the very essence of joyful and fulfilled living.

REVERENCE

"To revere" is originally an intensive form of "standing in awe" (Latin: *re-vereri*). Reverence is the attitude of someone for whom phenomena become transparent all the way to their innermost core, the awe-inspiring Mystery. This way of looking can be practiced and is characteristic of spiritually awake people. All creatures are rooted in Mystery and therefore deserve our reverence. We express this reverence by recognizing their dignity and acting accordingly. Today more than ever, our responsibility is to remember, honor, and care for the dignity of our natural environment and the human dignity of every person.

Rhythm

Getting in tune with the rhythm of the Great Dance is one of our key images for finding orientation. This image points to our great task to adjust all aspects of our life to the cosmic rhythm. Daily rituals can be a great practical help accomplishing that task. The mere awareness of the rhythmical sequence of daytimes and seasons is enough to pull us out of the humdrum of a hamster wheel and give our daily life a natural structure for joyful celebrations. Today, many people are rediscovering ancient rituals, like the monastic hours of prayer. They were, for centuries, the monks' way of attuning themselves to the cosmic rhythm and can inspire new forms of keeping in step with the Great Dance.

Ritual

Ritual together with doctrine* and morals* are three components of all religions. Ritual performances appeal to human emotions in an effort to reenact the encounter with Mystery. Rituals employ forms that allow the given culture, within which that particular religion is being founded, to celebrate Mystery as a present event. If, later in history, the cultural conditions change and the celebration of traditional rituals no longer arouses enthusiasm, that religious tradition will have to replace them with new forms that prove inspiring to people at that time.

Science

Scientific discoveries through worldwide cooperation and stringent peer-correction are among the greatest achievements of the human mind. Natural science offers us a magnificent picture of the world that can play an important role for finding orientation in life, as long as we remember that it is only half the picture. By its own definition, natural science restricts itself to exploring only the world of matter. Yet our inner experience has to be taken as seriously as our outer experience before we can investigate the world as a whole without prejudice.

In order to make the best use of science, we must learn to distinguish between well-established facts, theories built on the interpretation of those facts (with varying degrees of probability), and ideologies (in the negative sense of this word)—rigidly held theories blocking further exploration. Refusal to examine inner convictions in light of outer facts, and outer facts in light of inner convictions, will turn people into ideologists. We will want to take both natural science and the philosophical and mystical traditions of East and West, including shamanic and aboriginal traditions, into account in our search for orientation.

SELF*

SILENCE

Silence is one of two authentic ways for expressing inner stillness. The other one is word. To be an authentic word—not just chitchat—it must come out of stillness. But that stillness can also remain unexpressed. In that case, we experience it as silence. What matters in our spiritual life is inner stillness. Depending on the demands of a given situation, that stillness will come to word or express itself through silence.

What moves us so deeply when we hear the sound of a gong is its essential stillness. When we strike the gong, that stillness come to word, as it were.

We can learn to speak in such a way that our words express our inner stillness. The easiest way to do so is practicing silence. We will want to build periods of silence into our daily rhythm. That will allow us to experience stillness, even amid all the tumult and buzz that go on around us. We need such moments in which we let ourselves sink down into stillness until we become one with it. After that, it will not matter anymore whether we express that stillness through words or through silence. (See Mystery)

SOUL

When we say "I," we mean not only our mind. Our mind formulates the concept, but we need our body to express it. Thus, when we say, "I," we mean our "mind-body I" as an integral whole. This immanent wholeness has a dimension that transcends it. The Self transcends both mind and body. During ordinary consciousness, we are aware of that dimension of Self, but only peripherally; it is *as our mind-body I* that we are aware. During altered states of consciousness, however—for instance, in peak experiences—it is *as the Self* that we are aware and now our mind-body I is only peripherally included.

But why is it included at all? Because we know ourselves as participating in the Self, not as dissolving in it. And here is where the notion of "soul" comes in. My soul is what makes me irreplaceably distinct, even though I am fully participating in the Self that makes all of us one. If the Self were not one indivisible whole, we could say, the soul is our individual "share" in the Self. The term "soul" points to our sharing in that universal dimension without losing our individuality.

The soul is not something additional to our body-mind I, but another term for it. The international Morse code distress signal "S O S"—"Save our souls"—simply means, "Save us!" I don't have a soul, I *am* a soul. So, why do we use the term at all? It is a shorthand symbol, as it were, pointing to a paradox: our body-mind I is *mortal*, and yet it participates in the *immortal* Self. The term "immortal soul" expresses this paradox and gives rise to speculations about an afterlife.* (See also Afterlife, Body, Mind)

SPIRIT

Our English word "spirit" comes from the Latin *spiritus*, which originally meant "breath, life-breath," and came to acquire the meaning of "aliveness"—vitality, the essence of life. Spirit is the very aliveness of our life. So we might start by looking closely at life and afterward apply what we find to Spirit—going from what we are familiar with to what we are asking about.

As long as we breathe, we have life. "Have life"?—what a strange expression. Do we have life, or does life have us? We can't even stop breathing at will. If we hold our breath too long, life makes us faint and keeps us breathing. If it is true that we have life, it's also true that life has us. Life is in us, and we are in life.

But what is life? Biology and medicine know a few details about how life is working, but neither science nor philosophy has any clue what the essence of aliveness might be. Not even the religions that seem to think that they can answer every question pretend to know what life is. Thus, in and through life, we encounter Mystery.

What, then, is Mystery? By "Mystery," I mean that which we cannot possibly comprehend intellectually, yet we can understand it. The distinction between comprehension and understanding is a most important one. We may not have reflected on the difference between the two, but we are familiar with it from our experience with music. No intellectual analysis can ever hope to grasp what music in its essence is, yet we can understand that deepest meaning of music by listening deeply and being moved by it. Our "being moved" implies that music must "do something" to us before we can understand it. And as it is with music, so with life: We cannot understand its mystery, except by allowing life to do something to us.

And what does the Mystery of Life do to us? Moment by moment, the chorus of life invites us to sing a note that is in tune with all the other singers. If we do that, singing in a choir, the music comes fully alive, the performance is *spirited*, as we say. Life in fullness is like the Hallelujah Chorus in a sing-along performance of Handel's *Messiah*. A lively performance will embody the spirit of that chorus more inspiringly than a mediocre one. Choir, orchestra, and conductor together must attune themselves not only to each other but above all to the spirit of that piece in order to express it clearly and convincingly. They do not invent the spirit of the "Hallelujah Chorus." It has a life of its own. The performance merely lets that life become sound. It was there before its first note sounded, and it is there after the sound dies down. It exists beyond time. In fact, it would exist even if Handel's score had never been performed. But score as well as performance are merely ways to express the spirit of that piece, its inner life.

What we found to be true about life applies also to the spirit. Just as life is in us, and we are in life, so "we live and move and have our being" in the spirit. As life is mystery, so spirit is mystery. Just as we cannot comprehend life intellectually, but understand it by attuning ourselves to its chorus, so we can't grasp what spirit is, but understand it by coming alive in it. The spirit is the full aliveness of our body. We embody spirit, as a performance of the "Hallelujah Chorus" embodies the spirit of that piece. Just as the spirit of that Hallelujah is not affected, when the music ends, so, even when our time is up and our body dies, our spirit lives.

What our life in the spirit beyond time and space might be like, that is a question I cannot answer—as little as a caterpillar could tell what life as a butterfly might be like.

Spirituality

Spirituality is not a separate realm, but it characterizes every aspect of human life. Related to the Latin word *spiritus* (meaning life breath), spirituality is our aliveness. But aliveness has degrees—all of us know this from experience when we compare our aliveness in the morning and in the evening. Spirituality, likewise, has degrees, depending on its intensity and on how many areas of life are truly awake. The goal is aliveness in all areas of body and mind—from healthy living habits to respectful ways of treating others, to caring for our environment, and relating to Mystery.* For all this we need skills.

Our spiritual skills—intellectual, emotional, attitudinal, and so on—can be trained and improved through practices that make us more awake, alert, and alive. Spiritual training aims at the highest aliveness. That is why interaction with Mystery, the central task of human life, is at the core of spirituality. The more we wake up and come alive, the more we become aware of our encounter with Mystery in everything we experience. In this respect, spirituality is synonymous with religiousness. (See also Religiousness)

STILLNESS

Stillness is not identical with silence. The opposite of silence is sound or word. But the opposite of stillness is turbulence. Stillness is a calm, trusting, unperturbed composure of the heart. This inner stillness knows two ways of expressing itself: not only through silence, but also through word. Thus, a heart that has acquired stillness can choose to speak out or to remain silent, depending on what life demands at the moment. The right word, at the right time, will be a word that does not break the silence but lets the inner stillness come to word.

Inner stillness can be learned through practice. Stopping now and then, just long enough to take a few deep breaths, is a good start. The more we learn to quiet our own inner turbulence, the less external commotion can disturb us. People, centered in their inner stillness, radiate calm even when they are engaged in intense activity. They are like surfers, able to keep a steady balance amid swirling waters, by finding again and again their center of gravity. For stillness is not static. On the contrary, it results when dynamism reaches its peak—as when a hummingbird's wings are moving so fast that they seem to stand still, or planets zoom through space in perfect stillness.

STOP! LOOK! GO!*

SYSTEM, THE*

TAOISM

The *Tao-Te-Ching*, the most representative book of Taoism, written in sixth century BC, says, "The Tao that can be put into words is not the true Tao." The image of the Watercourse Way* conveys its essence better than words.

When we compare the world's religious or philosophical traditions, Taoism seems to be closer to basic human religiousness than any of the others. This is the reason that the *Tao-Te-Ching* has become so helpful and important a guide to many seekers today.

TIME

Time is often viewed as an irreversible movement, a movement that tends to ever greater diminishment: "time is running out," as if a bucket is leaking until it is empty. A key example for the movement of time is energy bound toward entropy. Viewed positively, however, time is a sequence of ever-new opportunities flowing toward us—a series of presents that are given to us in the present moment, the now, the "fullness of time."

TRUST IN LIFE

Trust in Life is our inborn attitude. Distrust, on the other hand, is an intellectual stance acquired only later. Distrust stands in constant contradiction to our actual behavior. We eat our breakfast and trust the life processes in our body to digest it—a task that we could never accomplish by conscious effort. In the same way, we trust—mostly unconsciously—all the otherwise workings of life, without which we could not continue living for a moment.

We say that *we have life*, and this is true—we experience our aliveness. But it is equally true to say that *life has us*—has us in its arms, like a loving mother. We have every reason to trust life. There is a deep truth to John Lennon's quip "Life is what happens while you are busy making other plans." And in retrospect (though usually not at the moment) we realize life knew better than our little mind what we needed. In this way, openness to our own experience confirms our right to trust in life.

Since trust in life is our original mental state and birthright, fearful distrust causes the turmoil of an inner contradiction. To be torn inside between trust and fear can cause serious mental and even physical harm. Healthy trust in life, on the other hand, rests on the many proofs of life's reliability and builds on this foundation. To realize its wisdom, harmony, and beauty, we must, of course, look at the big picture and not allow ourselves to be distracted by details, even when they are so distressingly close to our skin that it's very hard to look beyond them.

If life in nature displays so surpassing a wisdom, should we not trust in that wisdom when life resists our plans? For both our physical and our mental life Marie Curie's insight holds true: "Nothing in life is to be feared, it is only to be understood. Now is the time to understand more, so that we may fear less." (See also Fear, Science)

UNDERSTANDING

In sloppy colloquial speech we often use "understanding" and "comprehending" interchangeably. In fact, however, these are two quite different forms of intellectual perception. They spring from two diametrically opposed attitudes. In order to comprehend, we must reach out and take hold of the content we want to grasp. In order to understand, we make the opposite gesture, as it were, and allow ourselves to be grasped or gripped or moved. We are no longer in control.

The Western mind wants to be in control. Grasping comes naturally to us, while being moved frightens us a bit. "You are like people putting up an umbrella while taking a shower," says Eido Shimano Roshi. "You say you want to understand, but what you really want is to overstand."

In order to gain true insight, we have to practice both grasping and being grasped and learn to integrate the two. How much we can comprehend depends on the size of our grip. Thus, it remains always partial. But what grips us is limitless reality—ultimately rooted in mystery. (See Mystery)

UNDERSTANDING-BY-DOING

Every teacher knows how quickly children understand what they hear. They might remember a little longer what they get to see. But only the doing of what they are being taught can help them understand it from within and leave a lasting impression. This principle proves true not only in the classroom but in every aspect of Life. For Hinduism* and Yoga* in all its forms, understanding-by-doing is central. (See Mystery)

UTI/FRUI

These two Latin words—to *use* and to *enjoy*—constitute an important pair of concepts distinguishing two basic attitudes. We can use things and opportunities and we can enjoy them in many different ways. For our full aliveness, we need to learn and perfect both attitudes.

In practice, we tend to be preoccupied with the use of things and neglect enjoying them all too often in everyday life. Yet we do justice to the things and opportunities Life offers us only if we do not only use them, but appreciate all their qualities with all our senses and celebrate them as well. If we miss cultivating our enjoyment, use all too easily becomes abuse, quite apart from the fact that we deprive ourselves of a great deal of joy.

Violence

Violence is the abuse of power.

Vocation*

Watercourse Way, The

Watercourse Way, The, is a term that offers a beautiful and helpful image for the basic attitude of Taoism: the readiness to go consciously and willingly with the flow of Life. "Way" has in this context a double meaning: it points to the fact that the flow of Life has a direction and a goal, but also to the fact that the sage follows this direction to reach the goal, entrusting himself to the flow of Life—not, of course, like driftwood but like a swimmer.

Wisdom

Wisdom is a way of perceiving reality that combines comprehension and understanding—grasping and being grasped. We find this integrative approach among very simple people—wisdom from the mouths of children—but it also characterizes the most mature stages of the human mind. Holders of wisdom are reliable guides for knowing and doing, and authorities in the search for orientation. (See Mystery)

Word

Word, as a spiritual phenomenon, has two altogether different functions: it takes hold of a concept and at the same time puts us in touch with a depth far beyond that concept that must take hold of us in order to be understood. Thus, it is as if a word were making two diametrically opposed movements at the same time. For this paradox, we might use the image of a hand closed to grasp and, at the same time, open to receive. The closed hand stands for the prose function of a word, the open hand for its poetic dimension. Working for a scientific purpose, we use a word to capture a concept; in the play of poetry, we may enjoy the same word as a messenger of meaning. We can come to be aware of these two dimensions simultaneously. Then we can use and enjoy word both to grasp and to understand, and so realize the full power of words.

The power of words, however, comes to light also in a different way (often painfully so): once we have spoken a word, we cannot call it back, cannot reverse what it has set in motion. This is one of the reasons why it is important to learn to practice silence—until the right moment has come for the right word to be spoken. (See also Mystery)

WORK (SEE MEANING/PURPOSE)

YOGA

Yoga is an umbrella term that covers all the different spiritual paths of Hinduism. Hatha Yoga with its *asanas*—meditative body positions—is only one of these paths, although the best known in the West. The essence of yoga is connection. The very word "yoga"—related to the English word "yoke"—suggests connection, as for instance between two oxen under one yoke.

Yoga connects word and silence and leads to understanding. At every moment, Life speaks to us a "word" in the widest sense. If we listen so deeply to that word that it takes hold of us, it will lead us to do something in response. Only in carrying out this response by obedient doing will we truly understand, for the doing will lead us back into silence. Thus, yoga leads to understanding by yoking together word and silence.

YOU*

Index of Names

CPSIA information can be obtained
at www.ICGtesting.com
Printed in the USA
LVHW020620240523
747852LV00002B/332

9 781626 985155